Developing with Google+

Jennifer Murphy

O'REILLY®

Beijing · Cambridge · Farnham · Köln · Sebastopol · Tokyo

Developing with Google+

by Jennifer Murphy

Published by O'Reilly Media, Inc., 1005 Gravenstein Highway North, Sebastopol, CA 95472.

O'Reilly books may be purchased for educational, business, or sales promotional use. Online editions are also available for most titles (*http://my.safaribooksonline.com*). For more information, contact our corporate/institutional sales department: 800-998-9938 or *corporate@oreilly.com*.

Editors: Mike Loukides and Meghan Blanchette	**Cover Designer:** Randy Comer
Production Editor: Holly Bauer	**Interior Designer:** David Futato
Proofreader: Christie Rears	**Illustrator:** Rebecca Demarest

Revision History for the First Edition:

2012-09-07   First release

See *http://oreilly.com/catalog/errata.csp?isbn=9781449312268* for release details.

ISBN: 978-1-449-31226-8

[LSI]

1347046436

Table of Contents

Preface

Conventions Used in This Book

The following typographical conventions are used in this book:

Italic
> Indicates new terms, URLs, email addresses, filenames, and file extensions.

`Constant width`
> Used for program listings, as well as within paragraphs to refer to program elements such as variable or function names, databases, data types, environment variables, statements, and keywords.

`Constant width bold`
> Shows commands or other text that should be typed literally by the user.

`Constant width italic`
> Shows text that should be replaced with user-supplied values or by values determined by context.

 This icon signifies a tip, suggestion, or general note.

 This icon indicates a warning or caution.

Using Code Examples

This book is here to help you get your job done. In general, you may use the code in this book in your programs and documentation. You do not need to contact us for permission unless you're reproducing a significant portion of the code. For example, writing a program that uses several chunks of code from this book does not require permission. Selling or distributing a CD-ROM of examples from O'Reilly books does require permission. Answering a question by citing this book and quoting example code does not require permission. Incorporating a significant amount of example code from this book into your product's documentation does require permission.

We appreciate, but do not require, attribution. An attribution usually includes the title, author, publisher, and ISBN. For example: "*Developing with Google+* by Jennifer Murphy (O'Reilly). Copyright 2012 Jennifer Murphy, 978-1-449-31226-8."

If you feel your use of code examples falls outside fair use or the permission given above, feel free to contact us at *permissions@oreilly.com*.

Safari® Books Online

Safari Books Online (*www.safaribooksonline.com*) is an on-demand digital library that delivers expert content in both book and video form from the world's leading authors in technology and business.

Technology professionals, software developers, web designers, and business and creative professionals use Safari Books Online as their primary resource for research, problem solving, learning, and certification training.

Safari Books Online offers a range of product mixes and pricing programs for organizations, government agencies, and individuals. Subscribers have access to thousands of books, training videos, and prepublication manuscripts in one fully searchable database from publishers like O'Reilly Media, Prentice Hall Professional, Addison-Wesley Professional, Microsoft Press, Sams, Que, Peachpit Press, Focal Press, Cisco Press, John Wiley & Sons, Syngress, Morgan Kaufmann, IBM Redbooks, Packt, Adobe Press, FT Press, Apress, Manning, New Riders, McGraw-Hill, Jones & Bartlett, Course Technology, and dozens more. For more information about Safari Books Online, please visit us online.

How to Contact Us

Please address comments and questions concerning this book to the publisher:

O'Reilly Media, Inc.
1005 Gravenstein Highway North
Sebastopol, CA 95472
800-998-9938 (in the United States or Canada)
707-829-0515 (international or local)
707-829-0104 (fax)

We have a web page for this book, where we list errata, examples, and any additional information. You can access this page at *http://oreil.ly/dev_w_google_plus*.

To comment or ask technical questions about this book, send email to *bookquestions@oreilly.com*.

For more information about our books, courses, conferences, and news, see our website at *http://www.oreilly.com*.

Find us on Facebook: *http://facebook.com/oreilly*

Follow us on Twitter: *http://twitter.com/oreillymedia*

Watch us on YouTube: *http://www.youtube.com/oreillymedia*

Acknowledgments

Writing a book is a huge undertaking. I had lots of help along the way. There is no way that I can cover everyone who helped me, but here's a list of a few individuals who I would like to thank.

Thanks to all of my coworkers at Google for their technical reviews including Will Norris, Eric Li, Brett Morgan, Gus Class, and the rest of the Google+ platform team. Thanks to my friends at O'Reilly, especially Mike Loukides and Meghan Blanchette, who guided me through the process. Thanks to everyone who offered support in ways other than code, including my teammates from the Peninsula Roller Girls, who were always by my side, Jordan Robinson, for her wonderful and potentially disastrous recipes, and my partner in crime, Winona Tong, for creating the Baking Disasters logo and so much more.

CHAPTER 1

Introduction

Hello there! Since you're reading these words, the Google+ platform has probably sparked your interest. Maybe you have a killer app in mind, or perhaps you're just interested in learning what's available. Either way, by the time you're finished with this book, you will be comfortable digging into Google+.

The Google+ platform has three categories of features. Each of these categories is capable of standing alone, but things become more interesting when you combine them. These categories form a natural division, so we'll be going through them one at a time.

This means you can skip around from chapter to chapter if you wish. Once you become familiar with the components that you're most interested in, you will be able to combine them into the application that you're dreaming about. So, feel free to invoke a random access approach to reading this book. If you're more interested in REST APIs than publisher plugins, skip ahead. I promise I won't be offended.

The three categories of the Google+ platform are social plugins, like the +1 button, RESTful web services, which provide read access to Google+ data, and hangout applications, for writing your own real time collaboration apps. Additionally, the RESTful web services can be used in a couple of ways. You can either access public data directly when you know what you're looking for, or you can use OAuth 2.0 to access your user's data on Google+.

Since this architecture is a bit different from other platforms that you may have used, here are a few things that you may recognize and a few things that may be new to you.

Things You May Recognize

If you've developed on other social platforms you're in luck. Many of the technologies and techniques used in the Google+ platform are very similar. This is all thanks to a combination of open standards and best practices that have developed over the past several years.

Social Plugins: If you are a content publisher, or have an existing web application, Google+ plugins provide a simple way to integrate with Google+. They consist of Java-Script and small snippets of HTML markup. Google provides several social plugins including the +1 button, badge, share button, and sign-in button.

The JSON/REST/HTTP Stack: More sophisticated integrations with the Google+ platform rely heavily on JSON messages communicated with RESTful web services over the HTTP protocol. This is how you can programmatically communicate with Google+.

OAuth 2.0: The OAuth 2.0 specification is still in a draft state, but the need for secure access to user data is so acute that it is already being adopted by platforms across the Internet. Google+ has made a commitment to use OAuth 2.0 for APIs going forward.

Things That May Be New to You

As much as developing on Google+ is similar to developing on other modern social platforms, there are a couple of things that may be new to you.

Activity writes require user interaction: This is more of a philosophical difference than a technical one, but it will impact your designs.

A user's activity is a portal into the lives of people they know. A high-quality stream is very important to Google+. As a result, directly posting to a user's stream is not supported by the API. Instead, all writes must be triggered directly by the user. This is intended to keep the stream as high quality as possible. In practical terms this means that all writes must be made using the +1 button or the developer preview history API.

Preferred client libraries: RESTful APIs are great in that they provide a language-agnostic way to access data that resides on a remote system. Unfortunately, the specifications can be broadly interpreted, and nuance differences between implementations can make your code complicated.

To ease development in the language of your choice, Google is actively developing preferred client libraries for many popular languages.

If at all possible, use one of these libraries. Everything from the reference documentation to starter projects provided by Google is written using these libraries. In the same vein, all of the sample code is in this book is written using these client libraries.

The recommended client libraries are open source and provided under the favorable terms of the Apache 2.0 license.

Explore the API

Without further ado, it's time to dive into the API. The easiest way to see the Google+ platform in action is to use the API Explorer. This tool is accessible at *https://developers.google.com/apis-explorer/#s/plus/v1/*. It provides point-and-click access to most of the APIs that Google offers, including the REST APIs for Google+.

Follow these steps to fetch your public Google+ profile with the REST API.

1. Navigate to the API Explorer as shown in Figure 1-1. The hash fragment in the URL above should have automatically selected the Google+ API. Near the top of the content pane, you should see the selected API and version: Google+ API v1. Below this is a list of the available methods.

2. Scanning through the available methods, as shown in Figure 1-2, the `plus.peo ple.get` method looks like a match. Click it to reveal input fields.

3. Unfortunately, it requires a `userId`, which you probably don't know. The shortcut value `me` can be used in its place, but since your identity on Google+ is private information, it is protected by OAuth 2.0. You must authorize the API explorer to use it. Click the toggle switch entitled *Authorize requests using OAuth 2.0* to initiate this authorization.

4. An OAuth scope dialog will appear, as shown in Figure 1-3. Check the checkbox for the *https://www.googleapis.com/auth/plus.me* scope, and click the Authorize button. If this is your first time using the API Explorer with Google+ you must also grant the API Explorer access to your identity on Google+.

5. The API Explorer now has permission to determine your `userId`. Specify me for `userId` and to execute the query, as shown in Figure 1-4.

6. Upon execution, the request history pane at the bottom of the window displays the API Explorer's request and the API server's response, as shown in Figure 1-5. Assuming it was successful, you should see the HTTP headers from request and the full response. This includes a JSON representation of your public Google+ profile.

Congratulations! With a just few clicks you're already using the Google+ platform.

Over the course of these steps you witnessed many important features of the REST APIs provided by the Google+ platform. You danced the OAuth 2.0 dance to grant the API Explorer access to your identity on Google+, and you observed it fetching your Google+ profile.

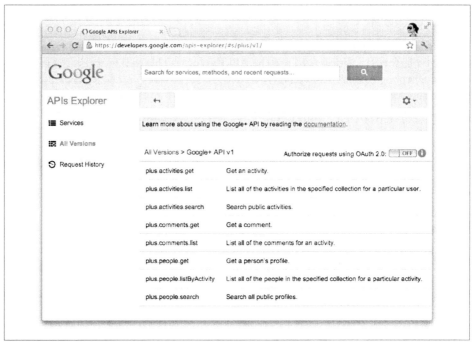

Figure 1-1. The API Explorer listing the methods of Google+ API v1

Figure 1-2. The API Explorer panel for crafting a people.get request

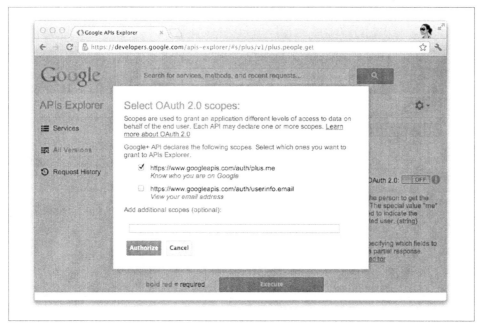

Figure 1-3. The API Explorer's OAuth 2.0 scope selection dialog for the Google+ API

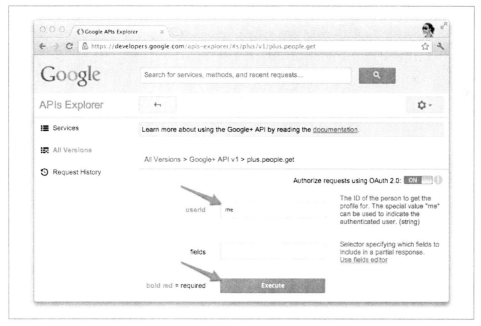

Figure 1-4. A completed people.get request form on the API Explorer

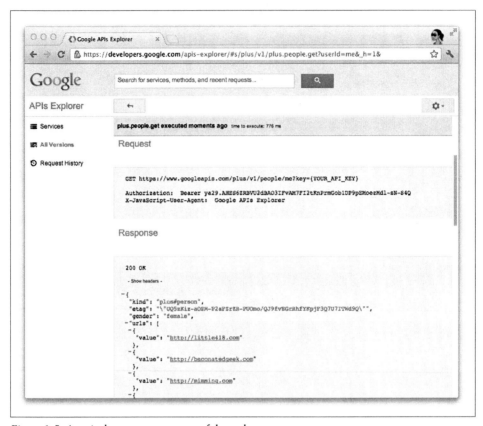

Figure 1-5. A typical response to a successful people.get request

CHAPTER 2
Social Plugins

In the introduction you used the API Explorer to fetch your public profile. If the REST API is the core of the platform, the plugins are portals into Google+ from your web presence. This chapter explores these social plugins.

Social plugins are snippets of JavaScript code and HTML markup. They can be easily added to existing web pages and applications with only a few lines of code. They are also highly configurable.

A great way to learn the social plugins is to use them. You will add them to a blog called Baking Disasters. Baking Disasters consists of a static HTML index page and two entry pages that describe a couple of particularly disastrous baking attempts. You can see the initial version of the blog here: *http://bakingdisasters.com/social-blog/initial/*. The entry pages are a great place to experiment with the +1 button, and the index is an ideal candidate for the Google+ badge.

The +1 Button

Before there was Google+ there was the +1 button. Announced at Google I/O in 2011, this feature predates every other component of the Google+ platform. It provides a one-click interface for your users to publicly identify their favorite content. Once users have +1'd a page, they have the option to share it on Google+.

From your user's perspective the +1 button is quite simple. They see your page, and since your content makes their eyes light up in excitement, they click the +1 button.

Figure 2-1 shows what happens next. The button turns red and their icon is added to the inline annotation. After this, the page is listed in the +1's tab on their Google+ profile, and their endorsement appears in annotations for this page. These annotations appear on your page as well in Google search result listings. Annotations are customized to the viewing user using their circles on Google+.

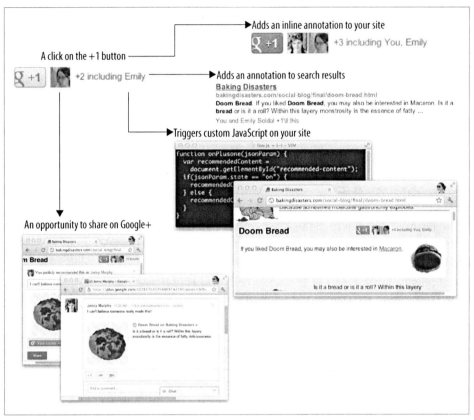

Figure 2-1. Some effects of a +1

After your user has +1'd your webpage, they will see the share dialog. It allows them to share your content on Google+. You can use structured markup to specify the title, description, and thumbnail image that are used.

Finally, the +1 triggers a custom JavaScript callback. This allows you to leverage their interest in creative and interesting ways.

Behind the scenes, a bit more happens. Many systems organize to provide this functionality. When the +1 button renders, information is loaded to provide your user a personalized annotation. When they click, a page fetcher visits your site in real time to extract your page's snippet: a short summary of your page. This summary is sent back to the +1 button, allowing the user to preview what they are about to share on Google+. Finally, when they share, an activity is posted to their stream.

Figure 2-2 illustrates this in detail.

1. The web page sources `plusone.js` from Google.
2. The web page renders the +1 button.

3. The +1 button fetches current +1 count.

4. Your user clicks the +1 button.

5. The +1 button communicates the click to Google.

6. Google fetches the target page.

7. Google generates a snippet for the target page.

8. The snippet is provided in the response to the +1 button click to preview the content that can be shared.

9. Your user shares the snippet for the target page on Google+.

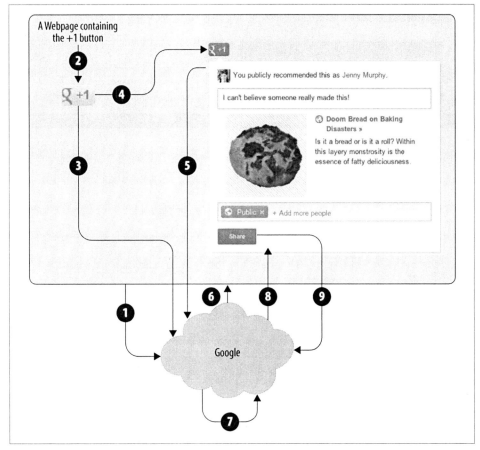

Figure 2-2. A communication diagram describing a typical +1 button render, click, and share

Adding the +1 Button

Now that you understand how the +1 button works, it is time to use it.

The +1 button is very easy to add to a web page. In its most basic form it requires only two lines of code. From this starting point you can further configure the button to match your needs.

The Google+ platform social plugins feature configuration tools. This is the best place to start. The +1 button configuration tool can be found at *https://developers.google.com/ +/plugins/+1button/*. The configuration tool, pictured in Figure 2-3, consists of a form, a preview, and a text area containing code. Play with the form. Notice that the +1 button and code automatically update.

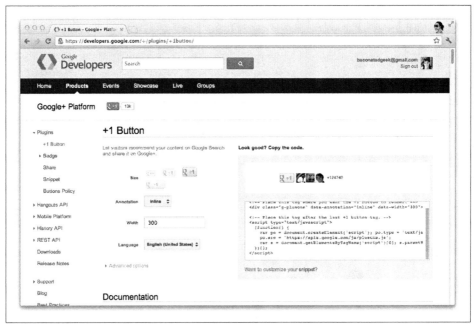

Figure 2-3. The +1 button configuration tool

Add the default +1 button to one of the entries on Baking Disasters. Copy the +1 button element into the place that you would like it to render. Based on the layout of the entry, a spot to the right of the header will work perfectly. Wrap the button in a `div` to float it right, as shown in Example 2-1.

Example 2-1. The +1 button markup

```
<header>
  <div style="float: right;">
    <div class="g-plusone" data-annotation="inline"></div>
  </div>
```

```
    <h2>Doom Bread</h2>
</header>
```

The +1 button markup is only half of the story, though. Paste the JavaScript into the page too. It can be placed anywhere on the page, including just before the `</body>` tag, as shown in Example 2-2. When it loads, it transforms all elements with `class="g-plusone"` into a +1 button.

Example 2-2. The asynchronous version of the +1 button JavaScript

```
</footer>
<script type="text/javascript">
  (function() {
    var po = document.createElement('script'); po.type = 'text/javascript';
      po.async = true;
    po.src = 'https://apis.google.com/js/plusone.js';
    var s = document.getElementsByTagName('script')[0]; s.parentNode.insertBefore(po, s);
  })();
</script>
</body>
</html>
```

Reload the page to see the +1 button, as shown in Figure 2-4.

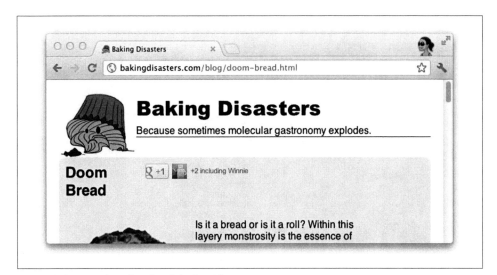

Figure 2-4. Doom bread with a default +1 button

The default width of 450 pixels has mangled the entry title. Sensible defaults are not always perfect for every layout. Return to the configuration tool and specify a width. Change the width to 250 pixels to leave room for longer titles, as shown in Example 2-3 and pictured in Figure 2-5.

Copy the updated code, and paste it into the entry.

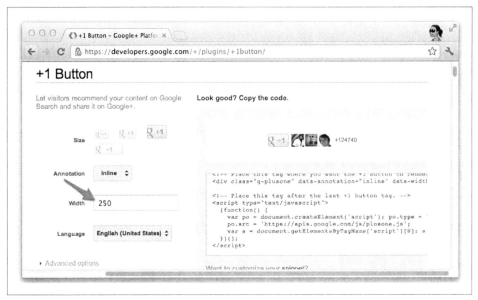

Figure 2-5. The +1 button configuration tool with the width explicitly specified

Example 2-3. +1 button markup configured to 250 pixels wide

```
<header>
  <div style="float: right;">
    <div class="g-plusone" data-annotation="inline" data-width="250"></div>
  </div>
  <h2>Doom Bread</h2>
</header>
```

Reload the page to observe the change. It should look like Figure 2-6.

Figure 2-6. Doom Bread with a +1 button configured to a width of 250 pixels

You can return to the configuration tool to explore the other options that it provides.

Customizing the +1 Button

The configuration tool provides a quick way to grab some code and run with the +1 button, but digging deeper unlocks more options.

The rest of the +1 button documentation can be found below the configuration tool. It documents all of the configuration options for the +1 button, including many that are not covered by the configuration tool.

For example, the documentation describes all of the tag attributes in detail. The annotation is pretty cool, but sometimes there isn't enough space. Scanning the documentation it appears that the annotation is configurable. The options include `inline`, the default, a smaller `bubble`, and `none`. Changing the annotation to `none`, as shown in Example 2-4, the +1 button shrinks to a much smaller footprint.

Example 2-4. +1 button markup with no annotation

```
<header>
  <div style="float: right;">
    <div class="g-plusone" data-annotation="none"></div>
  </div>
  <h2>Macaron</h2>
</header>
```

The floating `div` layout slides the smaller +1 button to the right as pictured in Figure 2-7.

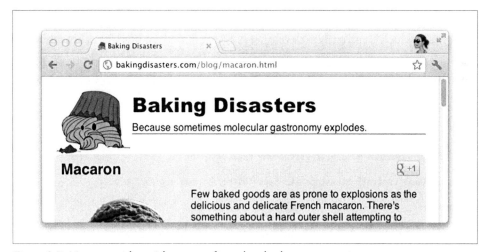

Figure 2-7. Macaron with a +1 button configured to display no annotation

There are many more parameters that you may find useful. Explore the documentation to learn about them.

Customizing Your Snippet

+1'ing a page creates content on Google+. It inserts a brief summary on the +1's tab of the user's profile, and an activity in their stream, if they share. The title, description and thumbnail image make up the snippet. You can customize your snippet to ensure that all of your pages look great on Google+.

By default the +1 button creates a best guess snippet. This is usually pretty good, but you know your content best. You can specify a much better snippet. The snippet can be specified using either schema.org markup or Open Graph tags.

Google recommends that you use schema.org markup to specify your snippet. Adding schema.org markup involves adding attributes to your existing content, so you do not need to add any new tags. It also allows top search engines, like Google and Bing, to parse your pages more easily.

Now that you understand why schema.org markup is a great solution, add it to a page. The first step is to select the correct schema. There's a handy list published at *http:// schema.org/docs/full.html*. It includes all of the schemas in one long page. In general, use the most specific schema that is appropriate to your content. It allows you to describe your content as richly as possible.

Scanning the list, it appears that there's a recipe schema: *http://schema.org/Recipe*. This is perfect for Baking Disasters. Add it to the macaron entry.

The recipe does not have content to match every single field in the schema, but it's wise to match as many as you can. The social plugins only understand the fields that are inherited from the thing schema, but complete markup provides the greatest benefits from search engines and future features of the Google+ platform. For example, the history API, which is currently in developer preview, makes use of many other schemas.

Add the `itemscope` and `itemtype` attributes to the parent element of the recipe, as shown in Example 2-5. On the macaron entry, the section element with class `content` is appropriate.

Example 2-5. Schema.org itemscope and itemtype

```
.Schema.org itemscope and itemtype
  <p>Because sometimes molecular gastronomy explodes.</p>
</header>
<section class="content" itemscope itemtype="http://schema.org/Recipe">
  <section class="post-body">
    <header>
```

Next, mark individual elements by adding `itemprop` attributes. Start with the properties inherited from the thing schema—`description`, `image`, `name`, and `url`—and follow by marking up the recipe specific fields such as `ingredients` and `recipeInstructions`. The resulting code is shown in Example 2-6.

Example 2-6. Schema.org recipe markup on the macaron page

```
<header>
  <div style="float: right;"><div class="g-plusone" data-annotation="none"></div></div>
  <h2 itemprop="name">Macaron</h2>
</header>
<img class="baking-photo" src="images/macaron.png" itemprop="image">
<p itemprop="description">Few baked goods are as prone to explosions as the delicious
  and delicate French macaron. There's something about a hard outer shell attempting
  to hold back the pressure of expanding almond-flour-goo that's reminiscent of a poorly
  designed steam locomotive.</p>
<h3>The Recipe</h3>
<ul>
  <li itemprop="ingredients">1 cup powdered sugar</li>
  <li itemprop="ingredients">1/4 cup baker's superfine sugar</li>
  <li itemprop="ingredients">3/4 cup almond flour</li>
  <li itemprop="ingredients">3 egg whites</li>
</ul>
<ol itemprop="recipeInstructions">
  <li>Mix powdered sugar and almond flour</li>
```

Reload and +1 the page. Something slightly different happens: rather than using a best guess snippet, the +1 button reads the schema.org markup. See the improvement in Figure 2-8.

Schema.org markup is the preferred option for specifying your snippet, but other options are available. When schema.org markup is not present, the +1 button looks for Open Graph markup. Open Graph markup consists of `meta` elements within your HTML head. These meta elements specify details about your page. Using Open Graph may make more sense if you already have social sharing buttons from other services on your site that use Open Graph.

Open Graph is less expressive, but it is also simpler. Add elements to the HTML header of the doom bread page: `meta` tags with property `og:title`, `og:image` and `og:descrip tion`, as shown in Example 2-7.

Example 2-7. Open Graph markup on doom bread

```
<!DOCTYPE html>
<html>
<head>
  <title>Baking Disasters</title>
  <link rel="stylesheet" href="style.css"/>
  <link rel="shortcut icon" href="images/logo_favicon.png"/>
  <link rel="canonical" href="http://bakingdisasters.com/blog/doom-bread.html"/>

  <meta property="og:title" content="Doom Bread on Baking Disasters"/>
  <meta property="og:image"
    content="http://bakingdisasters.com/blog/images/doom-bread.png"/>
  <meta property="og:description"
    content="Is it a bread or is it a roll? Within this layery monstrosity is the
    essence of fatty deliciousness."/>
</head>
<body>
```

Figure 2-8. Top: The best guess snippet; Bottom: The schema.org snippet

As you can see, both of these methods provide a way to specify your snippet. Which method is best depends on the implementation details of your application.

Leveraging the Callback

You have learned a lot about the what the +1 button can do, but you haven't written very much code yet. This is about to change. The callback is a software hook provided by the +1 button.

The callback allows you to trigger your own JavaScript code when the +1 button is clicked. It can call any function in the global namespace. Just supply it as a parameter to the +1 button, as shown in Example 2-8.

Example 2-8. A simple callback and +1 button markup configured to call it

```
<script>function onPlusone(){ alert("Hello, world!"); }</script>
<div class="g-plusone" data-callback="onPlusone"></div>
```

This unlocks a lot of potential. When a user clicks the +1 button they have just indicated their interest in your content. This is a great opportunity to engage them further.

On Baking Disasters you can leverage the callback to recommend other content that the user might enjoy. When a user +1's the page you can reveal this recommendation. The recipe page seems like a great place to perform this integration.

On a more complex site the task of determining recommended would likely involve an AJAX call, but Baking Disasters is simple. It hosts only two recipes. The only option is to recommend the other recipe when the user clicks on the +1 button.

Include the recommendation in the page and hide it with CSS. When the callback executes, inspect the button state and reveal or hide the recommendation appropriately, as shown in Example 2-9.

Example 2-9. A JavaScript callback that reveals content when your user +1's your page

```javascript
function onPlusone(jsonParam) {
  var recommendedContent = document.getElementById("recommended-content");
  if(jsonParam.state == "on") {
    recommendedContent.className = "active";
  } else {
    recommendedContent.className = "";
  }
}
```

When the +1 button is toggled on, the recommendation is revealed. When the button is toggled off, it is hidden as pictured in Figure 2-9.

The main callback is the best place to add interesting functionality, but there are a couple other callbacks. These callbacks, `onstartinteraction` and `onendinteraction`, trigger when a user begins and ends their interaction. They are very useful if you have a Flash advertisement or video that appears on top of your +1 button bubble. You can use them to hide the flash content while the user interacts with the +1 button and reveal it again when their interaction ends.

The callback is where developing with the +1 button really comes to life. This is your opportunity to integrate the +1 button into your core features and connect with your most active users. Be creative and have fun.

Special Considerations for AJAX Applications

AJAX applications throw a bit of a wrench into the system described above. In general AJAX applications track state using hash fragments. Hash fragments are the part of the URL after the # symbol. For example, a user may enter an AJAX application at http://example.com/ and navigate to a view of their profile at http://example.com/!profile/123. During this navigation the domain name and path do not change. To clients that do not execute JavaScript, like web crawlers and the +1 button's snippet fetcher, these URLs appear the same even though they contain very different content for the user.

Figure 2-9. Clicking on the +1 button triggers the callback and reveals the recommendation in the bottom screen shot.

Luckily, this problem has already been solved. Several years ago Google published a technique to make AJAX applications crawlable. It is described here: *https://developers.google.com/webmasters/ajax-crawling/docs/getting-started*. Because the +1 button fetcher is similar to web search crawlers, you can leverage this existing solution.

When you specify the target page for your +1 button, target a URL that specifies the state in a GET parameter instead of a hash fragment. For example, when you render a +1 button on `http://example.com/#!profile/123` specify the URL target to be `http://example.com/?_escaped_fragment_=profile/123`. Your web server, of course, must be able to understand the GET parameter and respond with the correct HTML.

There are many ways to implement this functionality on your web server. One approach is be to replicate all client side JavaScript behavior server side. In doing so, the crawlable version of every URL will always render the exact same HTML as if it were navigated to via AJAX. This solution will provide the best user experience.

If replicating this functionality server-side is prohibitively expensive, you may want to consider HTML snapshots. Create HTML snapshots by using headless browser programs, like those used for testing web applications, to regularly generate crawlable versions of your pages. When a client requests the _escaped_fragment_ version of a page, your web server would then respond with the snapshot version. This technique is described in more detail on the previously linked guide to making crawlable AJAX applications (*https://developers.google.com/webmasters/ajax-crawling/docs/html-snap shot*).

Troubleshooting the +1 Button

Sometimes things don't work as expected. Sometimes the +1 turns pink and shows an exclamation point, as shown in Figure 2-10. This icon does not help very much on its own, but just behind the covers there are more details. Modern web browsers provide powerful JavaScript debugging tools such as Firebug for Mozilla Firefox and the Chrome developer tools.

Figure 2-10. The +1 button indicating an error after an unsuccessful +1 click.

If you see a pink +1 button, open up Chrome's developer tools and switch to the network panel. Inspect the request for rpc as shown in Figure 2-11. This is the back-end API request made by the +1 button. You should see more details in the response body.

You may see "Backend Error" in the response. This means that the Google servers, which generate the snippet, were unable to reach or parse your page. Since the error message does not contain details, this can be a challenging issue to troubleshoot. Here's a checklist of common causes.

Reachable webpage: Is your web page reachable from the Internet? If you're developing on `http://localhost`, or within a corporate intranet, the snippet fetcher cannot reach your page. Be sure to publish it somewhere that Google can access it.

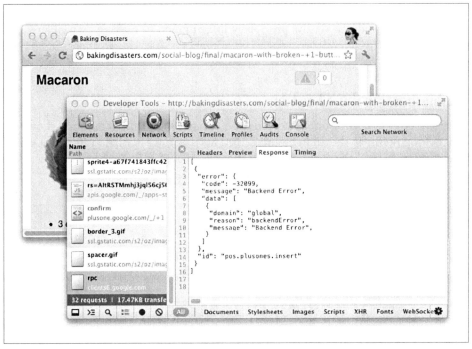

Figure 2-11. The +1 button's HTTP response inspected with Chrome Debugging Tools

Page response time: Since the snippet is generated in real time, your web server must be reasonably responsive. If page loads take more than a few seconds, you may encounter issues.

User agent filtering: The user agent of the snippet page fetcher is not part of the documented API. Do not filter, redirect or block traffic based on user agent.

Valid snippet markup: Paste the URL for your webpage into the Webmaster Central Rich Snippet Testing Tool found at *http://www.google.com/webmasters/tools/richsnippets*. This will fetch your page and validate your rich snippet markup.

Valid HTML: Does your website use valid HTML markup? Check it with a tool such as W3C's validation service: *http://validator.w3.org*. A few warnings and errors are probably fine, but the more errors your page contains, the more challenging it is to parse.

If you've gone through this checklist and you're still seeing an error when +1'ing your webpage, you can always reach out to the Google+ team for help. Flip ahead to the last chapter of this book to learn more about support. Do not forget to link to a place where the issue is happening.

The Badge

The Google+ badge makes it easy for you to advertise your presence on Google+ to visitors of your website. The badge comes in two flavors: one for user profiles and another for pages. Both of these badges link to you on Google+ and provide a way for visitors to add you to their circles from the badge itself, as pictured in Figure 2-12. The version of the badge for pages also includes a +1 button, consolidates the count of +1's from your Google+ page and homepage, and opens the door for Direct Connect.

Figure 2-12. Left: User profile badge; right: Google+ Page badge

Direct Connect allows visitors to navigate to your Google+ page directly from Google Web Search. Searches for the title of your page prefixed with a plus sign, such as +android for Android, will automatically forward to your page instead of listing search results. Additionally, since the leading plus sign demonstrates interest on the part of your visitor, they are automatically prompted to add your page to one of their circles, as pictured in Figure 2-13.

Figure 2-13. Entering a direct connect query into Google Web Search automatically takes you to a Google+ page and prompts you to add the page to a circle.

Adding the Badge

Baking Disasters is not a person, so you must use the badge for Google+ pages. Baking Disasters already has a Google+ page, shown in Figure 2-14, that you can use for the badge. If you don't have a page already, you can create one now. Follow the step-by-step tutorial to create one here: *https://plus.google.com/pages/create*.

Figure 2-14. The Baking Disasters Google+ page in all its glory

Now that you have both pieces, a homepage and a Google+ page, you can set up the badge. Just like the +1 button, the badge provides a configuration tool that is accessible at *https://developers.google.com/+/plugins/badge/* and shown in Figure 2-15. Several more advanced configuration options are documented below. Use the configuration tool to add a page badge to the index page.

Unlike the +1 button, the badge needs to know the page or profile that it links to. The configuration tool has a drop-down that lists your Google+ profile and the pages you manage.

Alternatively, if you are creating a badge for a page that you do not manage, or for a profile that is not yours, use the *other* option to specify the badge target by copying and pasting the URL as shown in Figure 2-16 and Figure 2-17.

Just like the +1 button configuration tool, the badge configuration tool automatically produces a preview and source code. The default badge is a bit large for Baking Disasters, but with a few clicks you can make it smaller. A small badge with a width of 170 pixels should fit nicely into the header. This configuration is shown in Figure 2-18.

Figure 2-15. The badge configuration tool

Figure 2-16. Copy and paste the numeric ID from your page URL into the badge configuration tool

The code for the badge has a two parts: JavaScript and HTML markup. The JavaScript portion probably looks familiar; it's the exact same code that renders the +1 button. You only need to include it once, so if you have any other Google+ plugin already on your page, you can ignore it. Next, the HTML markup must be placed where you would like the badge to render.

Here's the updated index page with the badge source in Example 2-10 and a screenshot of the rendered badge in Figure 2-19.

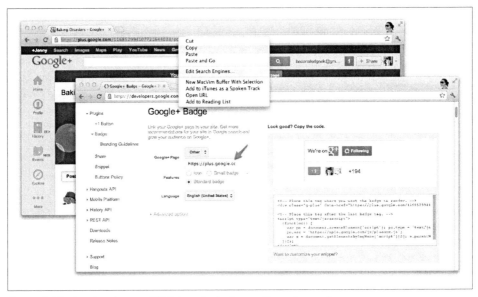

Figure 2-17. Copying the page URL into the badge configuration tool

Figure 2-18. The badge code configured for placement in the Baking Disasters index page header

Figure 2-19. The badge rendered on Baking Disasters

Example 2-10. The Baking Disasters blog index page: now with a Google+ badge in the header

```
<header class="blog-header">
  <div class="header-badge">
    <div class="g-plus" data-width="171"
      data-href="//plus.google.com/116852994107721644038?rel=publisher"></div>
  </div>
  <a href="index.html">
    <img id="blog-logo" src="images/logo.png" /></a>
  <h1>Baking Disasters</h1>
  <p>Because sometimes molecular gastronomy explodes.</p>
</header>
...
<!-- Asynchronously load the +1 button JavaScript -->
<script type="text/javascript">
  (function() {
    var po = document.createElement('script');
    po.type = 'text/javascript'; po.async = true;
    po.src = 'https://apis.google.com/js/plusone.js';
    var s = document.getElementsByTagName('script')[0];
    s.parentNode.insertBefore(po, s);
  })();
</script>
</body>
</html>
```

With the badge installed, visitors can now discover Baking Disasters on Google+ and add its Google+ page to one of their circles.

Performance Tuning Social Plugins

Social plugins add a lot of value, but this value comes at a small cost. They load and execute JavaScript code. This additional code can slow down page loads and reduce the quality of your user's experience. Luckily, there is a bag of tricks to pull from to mitigate this. These tricks work for any social plugin.

Asynchronous Loading

You may already be using asynchronous loading. The configuration tools supply you with asynchronous code by default. Asynchronous loading delays the rendering of all plugins until later in the page load, which makes pages feel more responsive.

If you are using this JavaScript to load your plugins, as shown in Example 2-11:

Example 2-11. Synchronous +1 button JavaScript code

```
<script src="https://apis.google.com/js/plusone.js"></script>
```

change it to this code, as shown in Example 2-12:

Example 2-12. Asynchronous +1 button JavaScript code

```
<script>
  (function() {
    var po = document.createElement('script'); po.type = 'text/javascript';
    po.async = true;
    po.src = 'https://apis.google.com/js/plusone.js';
    var s = document.getElementsByTagName('script')[0]; s.parentNode.insertBefore(po, s);
  })();
</script>
```

To take this philosophy one step further, you can even delay the execution of the asynchronous loader until after most of your page has been downloaded and parsed. Move the asynchronous JavaScript to the bottom of your page just before the closing </body> tag.

Explicit Rendering

By default the social plugins search the entire page for placeholder elements, such as <g:plusone>, <g:plus> and <div class="g-plus"></div>, and replace them with the plugins. If your page is very large, this may be inefficient.

You can reduce the size of this search with explicit rendering. When you source the JavaScript use a special piece of JSON to prevent the initial page scan. The responsibility of rendering now falls on you, but along with this responsibility comes the power to specify exactly where to render the plugins. Code illustrating both the special JSON and the explicit rendering is shown in Example 2-13.

Example 2-13. Explicit +1 button rendering

```html
<!DOCTYPE html>
<html>
<head>
  <title>Baking Disasters</title>
  <link rel="stylesheet" href="style.css" />
  <script type="text/javascript"
    src="https://apis.google.com/js/plusone.js">
    {parsetags: 'explicit'}
  </script>
</head>
<body>
...
<section class="content">
  <section class="post-summary" id="macaron">
    <div class="g-plusone"
      data-href="http://bakingdisasters.com/social-blog/final/macaron.html">
</div>
    <header><h2>Macaron</h2></header>
...
</footer>
<script type="text/javascript">
  gapi.plusone.go("macaron");
  gapi.plusone.go("doom-bread");
</script>
</body>
</html>
```

Using your own code to render the plugin has one caveat. You must load the `plusone`
`.js` file synchronously.

Delayed Rendering

If you have an extremely large number of social plugins on one page, you may want to
delay their rendering until the user interacts with elements near the plugin.

Specify a placeholder image for the social plugin and add a `mouseover` event handler to
content that the user is likely to mouse over, before they can reach the social plugin.
To keep this from being too jarring, use an image of the rendered plugin as a placeholder. Example 2-14 shows this trick being used on the Baking Disasters index page.

Example 2-14. Delayed +1 button rendering

```html
<script>
  function renderPlusone(placeholderId, targetUrl, origin) {
    origin.onmouseover = null;
    gapi.plusone.render(placeholderId, {"annotation":"none", "href":targetUrl}); ❶
  }
</script>
<section class="content">
  <section class="post-summary" id="macaron" ❷
          onmouseover="renderPlusone('plusone-macaron',
          'http://bakingdisasters.com/blog/macaron.html', this)">
```

```
    <div id="plusone-macaron" ❸
        style="width:38px;height:24px;display:inline-block;
        background-image:url(images/plusone_button_placeholder.png);">
</div>
    <header><h2>Macaron</h2></header>
    <p>Few baked goods are as prone to explosions as the delicious and delicate
```

❶ The JavaScript function, which replaces the placeholder div with a +1 button.

❷ Mousing over this section triggers the +1 button rendering.

❸ The placeholder for the +1 button.

When visitors reach the page they will see the placeholder image of the +1 button until they mouse over the recipe summary.

Can you see a difference between the left and right versions in Figure 2-20? If the answer is no, you're doing it correctly. The left browser window contains the placeholder while the one on the right contains the rendered button.

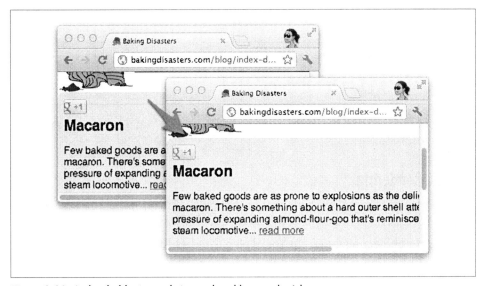

Figure 2-20. A placeholder image being replaced by a real +1 button

Use this technique only where necessary. Any image placeholder you use must be kept up to date as the plugins change. Also, no matter how perfect the placeholder image is, it will not be able to display annotations or existing +1 button state. If they have already +1'd your page, they will not be able to see it until they trigger the plugin to render.

Keeping Up to Date

There are always enhancements to the existing plugins and entirely new features being explored by the Google+ team. Before launching new features to everyone, they're tested with a preview group. If you'd like to stay on the bleeding edge you can join this preview group to gain early access to new features.

To join the platform preview group complete the form at *http://www.google.com/+/learnmore/platform-preview* with an email address for a Google+ profile. When new features enter publisher preview you will be notified via email at that address. You will only see publisher preview features while you're logged in to this account.

Platform preview is a great opportunity to experiment with features before full release. You can configure the new features, such as new display options, so only you can see them. Once the features enter graduate to full release they will automatically appear to all visitors.

CHAPTER 3

Public Data APIs

The RESTful data APIs are the core of the Google+ platform. These APIs provide read access to public fields on profiles, activities, and comments. Access to private data, specifically a user's identity on Google+, is controlled by OAuth 2.0, and API quotas are controlled by API keys.

The easiest way to gain an understanding of the public data APIs is to see them in action.

Integrating Google+ Comments

Baking Disasters is pretty cool, but do you know what would make it cooler? Comments would. Discussion can bring a blog to life, but sadly, they come at a cost. Not only do you need to worry about spam comments, but you also have to expose potentially sensitive software to the outside world.

Fortunately, the Google+ public data APIs expose the comments on your public activities. Since you're already sharing your blog posts to Google+, you can use JavaScript to render the comments from the activity right in the blog entry. Not only does this prequalify users to reduce spam, but it also allows you to keep Baking Disasters static HTML.

Experiment with the APIs

Before you start coding, spend some time to become comfortable with how the APIs behave. The API Explorer from the introduction chapter is perfect for this. You can find it here: *https://developers.google.com/apis-explorer/#s/plus/v1/*.

Use the API Explorer to trace the same steps that the comments plugin will follow.

1. Scan through the available methods in the API Explorer. The `comments.list` method, pictured in Figure 3-1, looks perfect. Unfortunately, it requires an activity ID.

2. Just above the `comments.list` method there is an `activities.list` method, pictured in Figure 3-2. This lists recent activities and provides their IDs.

3. Listing activities requires one more piece of information: your `userId`. The easiest way to determine your `userId` is to copy it from your Google+ profile URL, as shown in Figure 3-3. This technique works for both Google+ pages and user profiles.

4. Paste your `userId` into the `activities.list` form and select the `public` collection. Click execute to trigger the API call. The JSON response body renders in the history pane at the bottom of the page, as shown in Figure 3-4.

5. The response consists of some top-level attributes and a collection of activities within the items array. Each entry in the items array has an activity ID, as shown in Figure 3-5. Copy the ID for your most recent entry.

6. Switch to the `comments.list` method and supply the activity ID that you just copied, as shown in Figure 3-6.

7. Execute this request. The history pane now contains the comments associated with that activity, as shown in Figure 3-7.

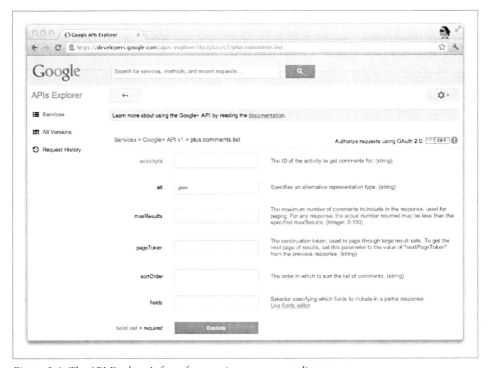

Figure 3-1. The API Explorer's form for creating a comments.list request

Figure 3-2. The API Explorer's form for creating an activities.list request

Figure 3-3. The location of the Google+ Page ID in the profile URL

Figure 3-4. The response from an activity.list request for the Baking Disasters public activity

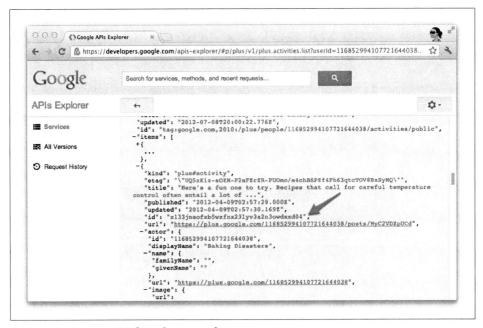

Figure 3-5. An activity ID from the activity.list response

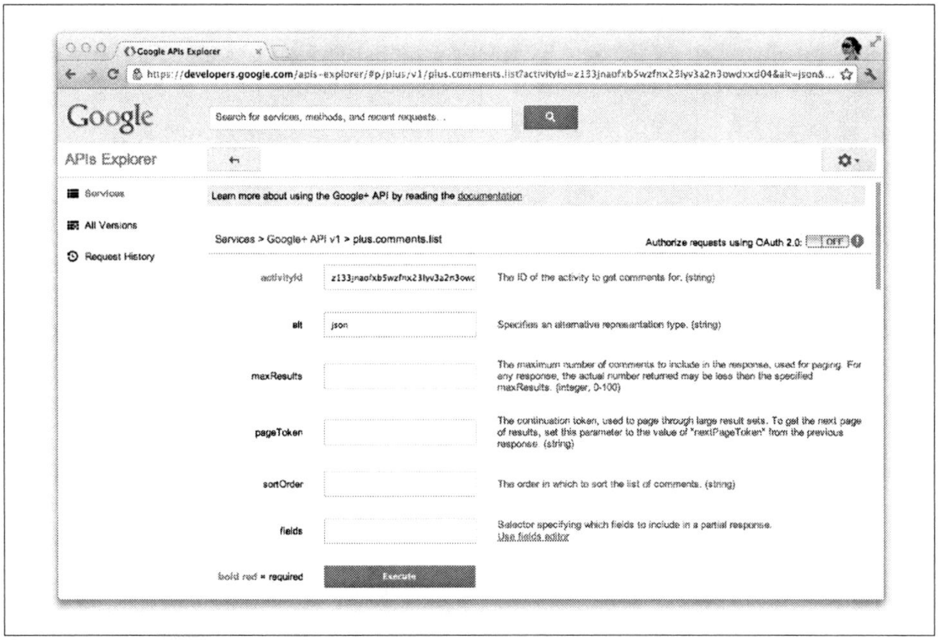

Figure 3-6. A comments.list request prepared with an explicit activity ID

Figure 3-7. The comments.list response for a Baking Disasters public activity

This flow that you just traced in the API Explorer is a reasonable flow for a comments plugin. Manually discover the activity ID for your activity on Google+, and use Java-Script to fetch and render the comments associated with it.

Client Libraries

Google probably provides an official client library for your favorite language. These client libraries make development against APIs faster by taking care of low-level tasks and providing you with an interface that embraces the development style of your language. You'll save yourself a lot of time by using the official client libraries.

The current library offering is shown in Table 3-1.

Table 3-1. Links to the Google API Client Libraries

Language	Project
.NET	*http://code.google.com/p/google-api-dotnet-client/*
Go	*http://code.google.com/p/google-api-go-client/*
Google Web Toolkit	*http://code.google.com/p/gwt-google-apis/*
Java	*http://code.google.com/p/google-api-java-client/*
JavaScript	*https://code.google.com/p/google-api-javascript-client/*
Objective C	*http://code.google.com/p/google-api-objectivec-client/*
PHP	*http://code.google.com/p/google-api-php-client/*
Python	*http://code.google.com/p/google-api-python-client/*
Ruby	*http://code.google.com/p/google-api-ruby-client/*

The comments plugin will use the JavaScript client library.

Registering Your Application

Before you can use the APIs to access public data you must register your application on the API console. This is how Google identifies the source of API calls and provision quota.

1. Navigate to the API Console on Google Developers: *https://developers.google.com/console*. Create a new project using the project drop down menu as shown in Figure 3-8.
2. Click "Services" in the API Console menu and toggle the Google+ API to "on," as shown in Figure 3-9.
3. Click "API Access" in the API Console menu to access the API key for your application, as shown in Figure 3-10.

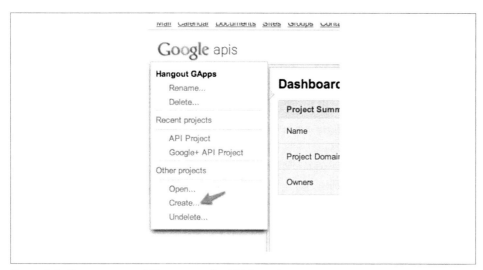

Figure 3-8. Creating a new API project in the API Console

Figure 3-9. Enabling the Google+ API

Figure 3-10. The API key as displayed on the API console

Time to Code

Just like the official Google+ plugins, the comments plugin renders comments within a `div` identified by a special class. It uses JavaScript to replace this placeholder `div` with the comments for that entry. Example 3-1 shows an example of a `div` element that the comments plugin will look for:

Example 3-1. The div element that will be replaced by a list of comments

```
<div class="g-comments-for z13zevjymuuge1zvl23lyv3a2n3owdxxd04"></div>
```

Create a new JavaScript file named pluscomments.js and include it into each blog entry. Edit the JavaScript file and create a namespace for your functions, and create a variable for your API key, as shown in Example 3-2.

Example 3-2. The comment plugin namespaced and configured with an API key

```
var commentr = commentr || {};
var apiKey = "AIzaSyA-H-eBvhWOyzjIJ2bWeaf1XAn855s8IRN";
```

To make calls you need an instance of the JavaScript API client. Load the client library with the name and version of the API and tell it your API key, as shown in Example 3-3. This function is automatically called by the JavaScript client library when it has finished loading and hence must reside in the global namespace.

Example 3-3. Bootstrapping the JavaScript API client library

```
function commentrLoad() {
  gapi.client.load('plus', 'v1', commentr.go);
  gapi.client.setApiKey(apiKey);
}
```

Next, find all of the g-comment-for divs and extract the activity ID, as shown in Example 3-4.

Example 3-4. Search the DOM for all of the g-comments-for elements

```
// search for g-comments-for classes
commentr.go = function() {
        var fetchElements =
         document.getElementsByClassName('g-comments-for');
        for(var i=0; i<fetchElements.length; i++) {
                var activityId = fetchElements[i].classList[1];
                commentr.fetchComments(activityId);
        }
}
```

Take the resulting collection of activity IDs and list the comments for each one. Each API response triggers the same callback function. Example 3-5 shows how to do this.

Example 3-5. Extract the appropriate activity ID, fetch its comments and insert them into the appropriate g-comments-for element

```
commentr.fetchComments = function(activityId) { ❶
  var request = gapi.client.plus.comments.list({
    'activityId': activityId,
    'maxResults': '100'
  });
  request.execute(commentr.parseComments); ❷
}
```

```
commentr.parseComments = function(responseJson) {
        var activity = responseJson.items[0].inReplyTo[0];
        var comments = responseJson.items;

        var insertionElements = document.getElementsByClassName('g-comments-for ' + ❸
     activity.id);
        var insertionElement = insertionElements[0];

        var newContents = "";
        for(i=0; i<comments.length; i++) {
                var actor = comments[i].actor;

                var commentBody = comments[i].object.content;

                newContents += "<dt><a href='" + actor.url + "'><img src='" +
                actor.image.url + ❹
     "' /></a></dt>" + "<dd><a href='" + actor.url + "'>" + actor.displayName +
     "</a>: " + commentBody + "</dd>";

        }
        insertionElement.innerHTML = "<dl>" + newContents +
                "</dl> <p class='g-commentlink'>Please comment on the <a href='" +
activity.url +
        "'>Google+ activity</a></p>";
}
```

❶ `fetchComments` is run for each discovered activity ID.

❷ Each response calls back to the `parseComments` function.

❸ Rediscover the place to insert the comment, since this information was lost in the chain of callbacks.

❹ Construct HTML for all of the comments and insert it into the document.

Finally, source the JavaScript client library and configure it to load the comments plugin. Source it in the entry pages and specify the `init` function to the `onload` parameter. Example 3-6 shows the macaron entry header with the client library added:

Example 3-6. Load the JavaScript API client library and execute the comment plugin's load function

```
<head>
  <title>Baking Disasters</title>
  <link rel="stylesheet" href="style.css" />
  <link rel="shortcut icon" href="images/logo_favicon.png" />
  <script src="pluscomments.js"></script>
  <script src="https://apis.google.com/js/client.js?onload=commentrLoad">
  </script>
</head>
```

Comments Integration in Action

That was pretty easy, wasn't it? Now let's see the comments plugin in action.

Use the API Explorer to discover the activity ID of your most recently public entry. For example, `z133jnaofxb5wzfnx23lyv3a2z3owdxxd04`. Return to that entry and add the placeholder `div`, such as the one in Example 3-7, that becomes the list of comments.

Example 3-7. A div element configured with an activity ID

```
<div class="g-comments-for z133jnaofxb5wzfnx23lyv3a2n3owdxxd04"></div>
```

Reload the page to see the rendered comments. It should look similar to Figure 3-11.

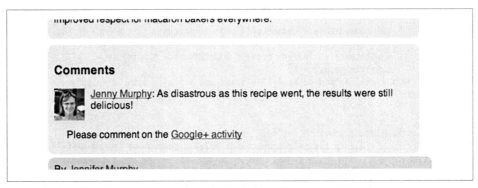

Figure 3-11. A Google+ comment rendered in the Baking Disasters web interface

What's Next?

The comments plugin is simple, but this simplicity comes at a cost. It's brittle and requires a hard-coded activity ID. A good companion to this plugin would be a tool that fetches your most recent activities and provides a placeholder `div` to paste into your entries.

OAuth-Enabled APIs

JavaScript plugins, like the comment plugin from Chapter 3, allow you to move beyond the official social plugins, but the depth of integration that they provide is limited. As you move on to deeper integration, some processing must be done server-side. To accommodate this, further examples are written in PHP. You will need to an environment capable of running PHP and a SQLite database.

The Google+ platform is not limited to PHP. You can find client libraries and starter projects for many popular languages including Java, Python, .NET, and Ruby. If Google does not supply an official client library for your language of choice, you may still use the REST APIs directly.

New Application: Baking Disasters 2.0

Baking Disasters is fun to publish as a static HTML blog, but as time passes visitors have started to express a desire to contribute their baking experiences. Being a social baker with a streak of PHP ability, this seems like the perfect opportunity to transform Baking Disasters into a social web application where everyone can contribute.

After one night of frenzied PHP hacking, Baking Disasters 2.0, as pictured in Figure 4-1, was born. It consists of an administration page for managing recipes and a public page for each recipe where visitors can publish their hilarious baking disasters.

Consisting of a couple hundred lines of PHP and a SQLite database, Baking Disasters 2.0 may not scale to millions of users, but it is a great starting point for further exploration of the Google+ Platform. Its simple architecture is described by Figure 4-2.

You can see the initial state of this application in action at *http://bakingdisasters.com/app-initial*. It's read only, for reasons that will become apparent shortly.

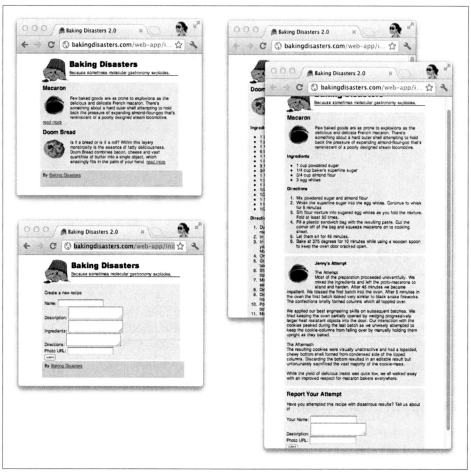

Figure 4-1. The screens of Baking Disasters 2.0. Upper left, index page for recipes; lower left, an administrative console to add new recipes; right, detail pages for each recipe that include user contributed attempts and a form to submit a new attempt.

Authentication Using Google+

Within hours of launch the site has been overrun with spam. Since visitors can post content without identifying themselves, the application is being abused. You must find a way to lock down Baking Disasters and protect it.

Fortunately, the Google+ platform provides APIs for identifying users. The REST API exposes public profile fields. It also allows visitors to share their identity with us via OAuth 2.0. This provides everything that you need to address the spam problem, without having to build your own user management infrastructure.

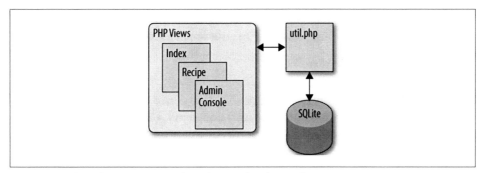

Figure 4-2. The Baking Disasters web application baseline architecture

OAuth 2.0

The Google+ platform uses OAuth 2.0 to authenticate users, and to authorize your access to their private data. Scopes control which data is accessible. When the user grants access, Google will provide your application with tokens that can be used to access your user's private data hosted by Google. Baking Disasters can use this to identify users as shown in Figure 4-3.

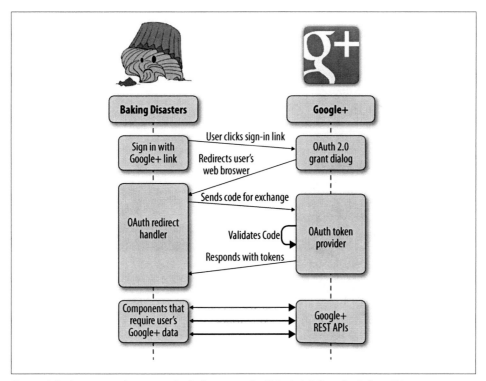

Figure 4-3. A sequence diagram, which illustrates the OAuth 2.0 flow for Baking Disasters.

Once a user's identity is known, you can use the REST APIs to fetch their public data. This includes their profile photo and their public activity on Google+. Additionally, their user ID makes a great user identifier in your application.

Accounts and API Keys

Your application must be configured on the API Console to use OAuth 2.0. Return to the Google API console to generate a client ID and secret. Use the client ID and secret to initiate the OAuth dance. They guarantee to the user that they are authorizing the correct application.

The client ID is publicly exposed during several steps of the authentication dance, but you should keep your client secret secure. If at any time your client secret is compromised you can return to this page to reset it.

Follow these steps to create your OAuth 2.0 credentials:

1. Navigate to the API console on Google Developers: *https://developers.google.com/console*.
2. Select your application from the drop down and click *API Access* in the menu.
3. Click on the large blue button shown in Figure 4-4 to create an OAuth 2.0 client ID.
4. Next, specify branding information for your application as shown in Figure 4-5. The product name and logo that you specify here are presented to your user on the OAuth grant screen.
5. Now for the tricky part. The OAuth dance requires you to specify the destination page, as shown in Figure 4-6. Google will redirect users there, once they have granted you privileges.
6. You should now see your client ID and secret, as shown in Figure 4-7.

Figure 4-4. The big blue button that you must click to create an OAuth 2.0 client ID

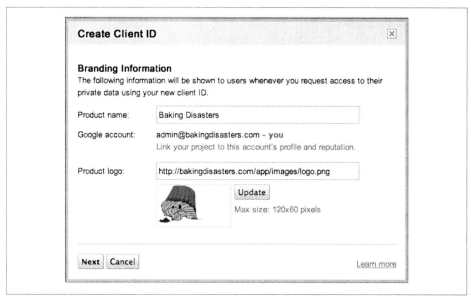

Figure 4-5. Creating an API client ID for Baking Disasters

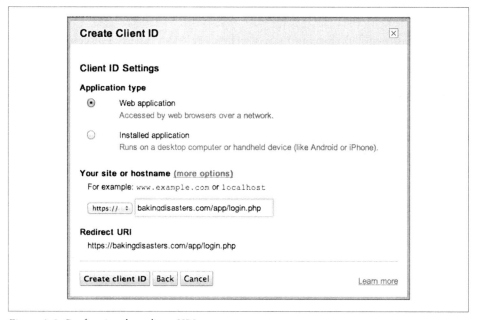

Figure 4-6. Configuring the redirect URI

Figure 4-7. The resulting client ID and secret

A Little More About OAuth 2.0

OAuth 2.0 is designed to solve the general problem of accessing user data that exists on a third-party system. This is a big problem to solve. Baking Disasters uses the basic flow for web applications that are running on a server. This flow is only a tiny sliver of the much larger OAuth 2.0 specification.

Not every application runs in a web browser. Applications that run as native code on a mobile device, or as a command line script, are also valid clients. To accommodate these applications OAuth 2.0 provides a variety of flows, each with their own nuances.

OAuth 2.0 is big enough that any discussion here can't do it justice. You can learn more about OAuth at Google here: *http://code.google.com/apis/accounts/docs/OAuth2.html*.

Starter Projects

Client libraries make development much faster in the long run. However, just like any other tool, they have a learning curve. It will take you some time to make the most of their time-saving features. To smooth out this potentially sharp learning curve, the Google+ platform provides starter projects for the most popular client libraries. They are listed in Table 4-1.

Table 4-1. Google+ REST API starter projects

Language	Project
Go	*https://code.google.com/p/google-plus-go-starter/*
Java	*http://code.google.com/p/google-plus-java-starter/*
PHP	*http://code.google.com/p/google-plus-php-starter/*
Python	*http://code.google.com/p/google-plus-python-starter/*
Ruby	*http://code.google.com/p/google-plus-ruby-starter/*

These aptly named starter projects provide you with a turnkey foundation for whatever you would like to write. All you need to do is download the starter project and add your application identifiers. Starting from working code makes further development much easier.

Baking Disasters is written in PHP, so the PHP starter project is a great place to start. Once it's working you can merge them together to start your Google+ integration.

1. Download the starter project from the downloads tab on *http://code.google.com/p/ google-plus-php-starter/*. Unzip the archive to reveal that the project contains three files, including a readme with usage instructions, as shown in Figure 4-8.

2. The readme opens with a description of the starter project prerequisites. Most PHP installations will include the cURL and JSON extensions. The only thing that you need is the PHP client library.

3. Download the PHP client library from *http://code.google.com/p/google-api-php-cli ent/* and extract it in the starter project's folder. You should end up with a directory structure that looks like Figure 4-9.

4. The readme instructs you to set up an application on the API Console to create a Client ID, Client Secret, and API key. Use the values that you set up for your API project in the previous section, as shown in Figure 4-10.

5. Use your favorite text editor to edit `index.php`. Scroll to about line 30 and paste these identifiers in the appropriate places, as shown in Example 4-1.

6. Next, update the `redirectURI` field to match the value in the API console and the place you'll be hosting this file. If you plan to run the starter project from a your workstation, this may be `localhost`.

Figure 4-8. The Google+ API PHP starter project's archive contents and readme file

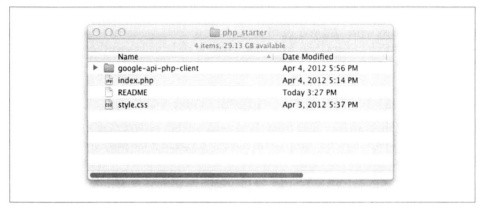

Figure 4-9. The PHP starter project with the PHP API client library

Example 4-1. The fully configured PHP Google+ API starter project

```
$client = new apiClient();
$client->setApplicationName("Google+ PHP Starter Application");
// Visit https://code.google.com/apis/console to generate your
// oauth2_client_id, oauth2_client_secret, and to register your oauth2_redirect_uri.
$client->setClientId('116363269786.apps.googleusercontent.com');
$client->setClientSecret('EJlqDrWkEYmmYznlken2JW-B');
$client->
  setRedirectUri('http://bakingdisasters.com/web-app/php-starter');
$client->setDeveloperKey('AIzaSyDrH_5j2-cPK7EZRANWjA6_g0xCZRrxH-U');
$client->setScopes(array('https://www.googleapis.com/auth/plus.me'));
$plus = new apiPlusService($client);

if (isset($_REQUEST['logout'])) {
  unset($_SESSION['access_token']);
}
```

It's ready to go. Deploy the starter project to your web server, and view it in a web browser. Figure 4-11 shows what happens next. You'll be greeted by a page that asks you to log in. Clicking the big blue link redirects you to Google's authentication service where you'll be asked to grant the starter project permissions to know who you are on Google. Click the *Allow access* button.

Having been granted access, the starter project now completes the OAuth dance. It exchanges a code for an access token. This token is used to make API calls, which are shown in Figure 4-12.

With only a few minutes invested you now have a self contained web application capable of making API calls to the Google+ REST APIs. If you run into issues as you progress you can always return to this code as a sanity check.

Figure 4-10. The client ID, client secret and API key on the API console

Bringing it Together

You now have two functioning applications: Baking Disasters, and the PHP starter project. Combine them to add sign-in functionality to Baking Disasters. This consists mostly of strategic copy-and-paste from the starter project into the appropriate places in Baking Disasters.

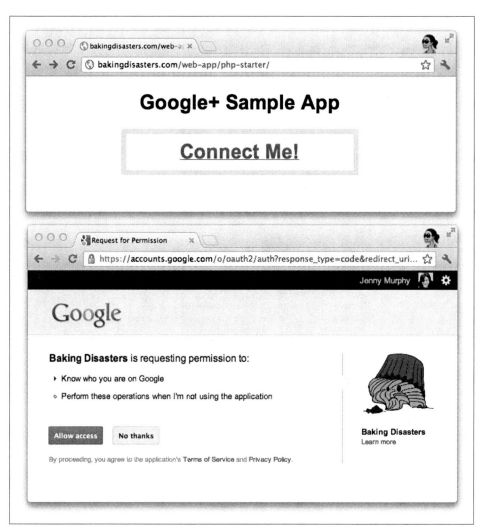

Figure 4-11. Top: The starter project landing page; Bottom: The permission grant page

Create new PHP files for the sign-in and sign-out operations and store the currently signed in state within PHP's session. Add code that's shared across multiple files, such as code to create or manage API clients, to `util.php`.

All of the pages in Baking Disasters require the use of an API client. Take the code from the top of the starter project and copy it into `util.php`, as shown in Example 4-2. Create a new function that returns a Google+ API client.

Figure 4-12. The completed flow of the starter project displaying your name, profile icon, and recent activity

Example 4-2. A PHP function that creates a configured API client

```php
require_once 'google-api-php-client/src/apiClient.php'; ❶
require_once 'google-api-php-client/src/contrib/apiPlusService.php'; ❷

session_start(); ❸

date_default_timezone_set('America/Los_Angeles');

function init_api_client() ❹
{
  global $app_base_path;

  $client = new apiClient();
  $client->setApplicationName("Baking Disasters");
  $client->setClientId('116363269786.apps.googleusercontent.com');
  $client->setClientSecret('EJlqDrWkEYmmYznlken2JW-B');
  $client->setRedirectUri($app_base_path . '/login.php');
  $client->setDeveloperKey('AIzaSyDrH_5j2-cPK7EZRANWjA6_gOxCZRrx');
  $client->setScopes(array('https://www.googleapis.com/auth/plus.me'));
  return $client;
}
```

❶ Load the core PHP API client library.

❷ Load the generated Google+ API client library extension.

❸ Start the session so that you have a place to store access tokens for your users.

❹ Create a new client library instance configured for your API project and server.

Next, copy the rest of the authentication logic into two PHP files: login.php and log
out.php. With a bit of shuffling login.php looks Example 4-3.

Example 4-3. Initiate an OAuth 2.0 flow from login.php

```php
<?php
include_once("util.php");
$client = init_api_client();
$auth_url = $client->createAuthUrl();
if(!isset($_GET['code'])) { ❶
  header("location: " . $auth_url);
}
else { //if (isset($_GET['code'])) { ❷
  $client->authenticate();
  $_SESSION['access_token'] = $client->getAccessToken();
  header('Location: '.$app_base_path);
}
```

❶ If the code GET parameter is not set, initiate a new OAuth 2.0 flow.

❷ If code is set, use it to complete the OAuth flow.

And logout.php looks like Example 4-4.

Example 4-4. Sign users out by deleting their access and refresh tokens from the session

```php
<?php
include_once("util.php");
unset($_SESSION['access_token']);
header('Location: '.$app_base_path);
```

With these files created add sign-in and sign-out links to the header of every page with
the code in Example 4-5.

Example 4-5. Sign-in and sign-out links for the header of each page

```php
<body>
<header class="blog-header">
  <span class="login">
    <?php if(isset($_SESSION['access_token'])) { ?>
      <a href="logout.php">Logout</a>
    <?php } else { ?>
      <a href="login.php">Sign in with Google+</a>
    <?php } ?>
  </span>
  <a href="index.php"><img id="blog-logo" src="images/logo.png"/></a>
  <h1>Baking Disasters</h1>
```

This implementation allows users to sign in and out, but it can already benefit from
some refactoring. Currently, signing in and out redirects users back to the index page.

Use the session and referrer header to return them to the page where they started. Example 4-6 is an updated login.php.

Example 4-6. Redirecting the user to the page from which they initiated the sign in improves their experience

```
// If there's a code we need to swap it for an access token
else { //if (isset($_GET['code'])) {
  $client->authenticate();
  $_SESSION['access_token'] = $client->getAccessToken();

  if(isset($_SESSION['original_referrer'])) {
    header('Location: ' . $_SESSION['original_referrer']);
    unset($_SESSION['original_referrer']);
  } else {
    header('Location: '.$app_base_path);
  }
}
```

Example 4-7 shows the updated logout.php.

Example 4-7. Also redirect the user to the page from which they initiated the sign out

```
<?php
include_once("util.php");
unset($_SESSION['access_token']);
if(isset($_SERVER['HTTP_REFERER'])) {
  header('Location: '.$_SERVER['HTTP_REFERER']);
} else {
  header('Location: '.$app_base_path);
}
```

The page header determines if a user is currently signed in by checking the existence of an access token in the session. Checking the signed-in state is something that many parts of the Baking Disasters needs, so refactor this into a utility function. Add this function to util.php, as shown in Example 4-8.

Example 4-8. A function that checks the current user's sign-in state

```
function is_logged_in()
{
  if (isset($_SESSION['access_token'])) {
    return true;
  } else {
    return false;
  }
}
```

And update the header of each page to use it, as shown in Example 4-9.

Example 4-9. Using the is_logged_in() function abstracts the session implementation out of your PHP pages

```
<body>
<header class="blog-header">
  <span class="login">
    <?php if(is_logged_in()) { ?>
      <a href="logout.php">Logout</a>
    <?php } else { ?>
      <a href="login.php">Sign in with Google+</a>
    <?php } ?>
  </span>
  <a href="index.php"><img id="blog-logo" src="images/logo.png"/></a>
  <h1>Baking Disasters</h1>
```

Locking Stuff Down

Now that users can sign in, you can restrict access to sensitive features such as the disaster submission form and the administration console.

Restricting the disaster submission form to currently signed in users is quite easy. Just add an `is_logged_in` check when you render the form in `recipe.php`, as shown in Example 4-10.

Example 4-10. Only display the report attempt form to signed in users

```
<section class="content attempt-form">
<?php if(is_logged_in()) { ?>
  <h2>Report Your Attempt</h2>

  <p>Have you attempted this recipe with disastrous results?
    Tell us about it!</p>

  <form method="post">
    <input type="hidden" name="recipe_id" value="<?= $_GET['id'] ?>"/>
    <label>Your Name: <input name="author_name"></label>
    <label>Description: <textarea name="description"></textarea></label>
    <label>Photo URL: <input type="text" name="photo_url"/></label>
    <input type="submit"/>
  </form>
<?php } else { ?>
  <p>Log in to tell us about your attempt!</p>
<?php } ?>
</section>
```

And when you insert into the database, as shown in Example 4-11.

Example 4-11. Only allow signed-in users to write to the database

```
<?php
include_once("util.php");
if ($_POST && is_logged_in()) {
  insert_attempt($_POST['recipe_id'], $_POST['author_name'],
                 $_POST['description'], $_POST['photo_url']);
```

```
  echo "<p class='notice'>Attempt inserted!</p>";
}
?>
```

Unauthenticated users are now asked to log in to share their attempts, as shown in Figure 4-13.

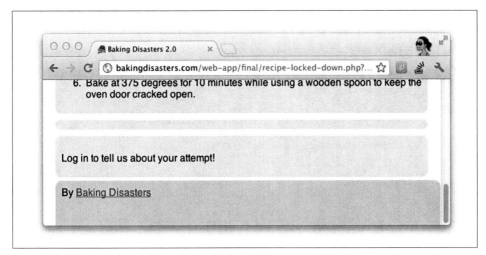

Figure 4-13. The logged-out view of the recipe page

This plugs up the biggest opening for spam, but what if someone discovers `admin.php`? They could insert new recipes. To ensure that only the site administrator, Jenny Murphy, can add new recipes, check to see if the signed in user has the correct user ID. To make this comparison fetch the signed in user's profile from the API.

The starter project shows us how to make this call. It fetches the current user's profile just after it validates that the current user has an access token. This call is shown in Example 4-12.

Example 4-12. Fetch the signed-in user from the API

```
$me = $plus->people->get('me');
```

Wrap this behavior into a `get_plus_profile` function, as shown in Example 4-13.

Example 4-13. A function that fetches the signed-in user

```
function get_plus_profile()
{
  if (!is_logged_in()) {
    die("Expected to be logged in here");
  }

  $client = init_api_client();
  $client->setAccessToken($_SESSION['access_token']);
```

```
    $plus = new apiPlusService($client);
    $me = $plus->people->get('me');
    return $me;
}
```

And then use the code in Example 4-14 to verify that Jenny is the user viewing `admin.php`.

Example 4-14. Check the signed-in user's profile ID to restrict access to admin.php

```
</header>
<?php
if(is_logged_in()) {
  $me = get_plus_profile();
  if($me['id'] == "102817283354809142195") {
    if ($_POST) {
      insert_recipe($_POST['name'], $_POST['description'],
                    $_POST['ingredients'], $_POST['directions'],
                    $_POST['photo_url']);
      echo "<p class='notice'>Recipe inserted.</p>";
    }
?>
<section class="content">
...
</section>
  <?php    } else { echo "Only Jenny Murphy can access this page.";  }}?>
<footer>
```

This prevents interlopers from adding recipes. Instead, they see the error message shown in Figure 4-14.

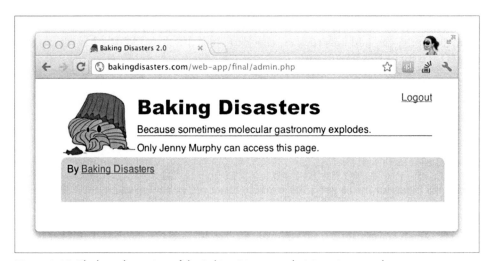

Figure 4-14. The logged-out view of the Baking Disasters administration console.

All writes to Baking Disasters are now protected, but there's so much more that you can do with Google+.

A Preview of the Sign-in Button

OAuth 2.0 is an amazing standard. It gives your users a way to share their Google data and identity with your application. Unfortunately, to support OAuth, you had to add quite a bit of code to your application. OAuth is complex, but implementing it does not have to be.

The Google+ sign-in button, shown in Figure 4-15, aims to make implementing OAuth easier. It accomplishes this by providing you with a plugin just like the +1 button. When the user clicks the Sign In button they are taken through an OAuth flow and the code is returned to your application. This replaces the first half of your OAuth code with a single line of markup, shown in Example 4-15.

Figure 4-15. Baking Disasters refactored to use the sign-in button

Example 4-15. Sign-in button markup

```
<g:plus action="connect"
    clientid="1234567890.apps.googleusercontent.com"
    callback="onSignInCallback"></g:plus>
```

The sign-in button is currently in developer preview. During this time, preview only works for developers who are enrolled in the preview. You can start experimenting with it, but you can't release software that uses it until the developer preview has finished. You should also be prepared for breaking changes at any point during this developer preview.

The developer preview is tied to a Google account. When you are logged in to Google with a developer preview account, the sign-in button will render. Use this form to sign up: *https://developers.google.com/+/history/preview/*.

Google Developers provides theoretical explanation, API reference material, and starter projects that use the Sign In button: *https://developers.google.com/+/history/*.

Making Baking Disasters Social

Baking Disasters now requires authentication for the creation of data. Authentication is useful, but it's neither very exciting nor does it add any new features to your site. Let's knock it up a notch and use the APIs to leverage even more features of Google+.

Import Disasters from Google+

Baking Disasters would benefit a lot from importing content from Google+. If users could import attempts from their recent activity on Google+ they can leverage the Google+ mobile application. They can live-share their baking attempt on the Google+ mobile application. Once the smoke has cleared and they return to their laptops, they can import content at their convenience. This flow is described in Figure 4-16.

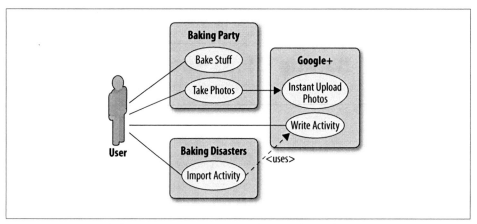

Figure 4-16. During the baking party the user takes photos and records activity on their cell phone; after the party ends, the user can import that activity from Google+ into Baking Disasters

Importing activity is a bit more involved than the previous enhancements. It will require you to add a new page to provide an import interface and update the recipe page to render imported attempts.

To comply with the developer policies, which restrict the storage of Google+ user data, you must store references to the activities on Google+ instead of the whole activity. This requires refactoring of your database. It also means that you must handle activities that have been deleted. However, it pays off in the form of automatically handling updates and edits. The resulting flow is shown in Figure 4-17.

The database schema changes are simple, but they do require a breaking change. Example 4-16 shows the new table creation statement. You can either run this by hand using the SQLite command line interface or delete the database and start from scratch.

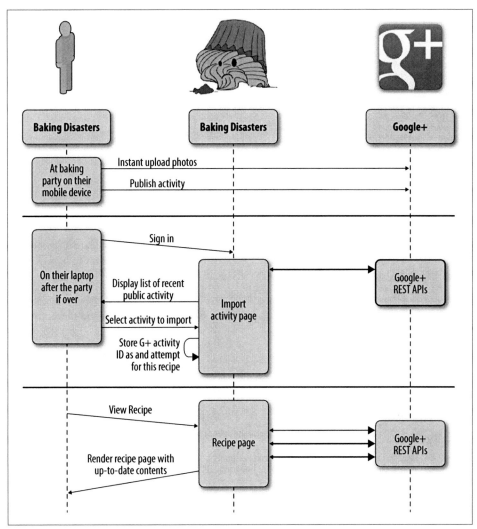

Figure 4-17. A sequence diagram describing what happens during the baking party, when the user imports activity into Baking Disasters, and when Baking Disasters renders the activity on the recipe page

Example 4-16. A new table schema for baking attempts

```
sqlite_exec($db, 'create table attempts (recipe_id int,
  google_plus_activity_id text);');
```

Just as in the previous enhancements most of the heavy lifting will be done by functions in *util.php*. Add a function that fetches a page of public activities for the currently logged in user. You can model this code from the activity list in the starter project. The resulting code is shown in Example 4-17.

Example 4-17. Fetch the signed in user's recent public activities from the API

```php
function get_recent_activities()
{
  if (!is_logged_in()) {
    die("Expected to be logged in here");
  }

  $client = init_api_client();
  $client->setAccessToken($_SESSION['access_token']);
  $plus = new apiPlusService($client);

  $optional_parameters = array('maxResults' => 20);
  $activities =
      $plus->activities->listActivities('me', 'public', $optional_parameters);
  return $activities;
}
```

Having changed the way activities are stored, you also need to update the way that you recall them, as shown in Example 4-18. The database only stores the activity ID. The rest of the fields must come from an API call to fetch each activity.

The fetch is a great time to clean up any activities that were deleted from Google+. If the API returns a 404, you know that the activity is gone and you should clean up the reference to it.

Example 4-18. This code fetches the activities associated with each recorded attempt for a specific recipe ID. If an activity no longer exists, it removes it from the database

```php
function list_attempts($recipe_id)
{
  $db = init_db();
  $recipe_id = sqlite_escape_string(strip_tags($recipe_id));

  $query = sqlite_query($db, "select * from attempts where recipe_id = '$recipe_id'"); ❶
  $attempt_stubs = sqlite_fetch_all($query, SQLITE_ASSOC);

  $client = init_api_client();
  $plus = new apiPlusService($client);

  $attempts = Array();
  foreach ($attempt_stubs as $attempt_stub) {
    $google_plus_activity_id = $attempt_stub['google_plus_activity_id'];
    try {
      $activity = $plus->activities->get($google_plus_activity_id); ❷

      $attempt = Array();
      $attempt['url'] = $activity['url'];
      $attempt['author'] = $activity['actor'];
      $attempt['description'] = $activity['object']['content'];
      if (count($activity['object']['attachments']) > 0) { ❸
        $attempt['photo_url'] =
            $activity['object']['attachments'][0]['image']['url'];
      }
      array_push($attempts, $attempt);
```

```
    } catch (Exception $e) {
      if ($e->getCode() == 404) { ❹
        // If it's a 404, it has been deleted by the user. Clean it up.
        sqlite_exec($db, "delete from attempts where
                        google_plus_activity_id='$google_plus_activity_id';");
      }
    }
  }
  return $attempts;
}
```

❶ Fetch the list of activity IDs for this recipe from the database.

❷ Fetch the full activity for each one using the Google+ API.

❸ Assuming that the first attachment is an image, extract it from the API response.

❹ Deleted activities return a 404. If you see one, remove the activity ID from your database.

This method returns a list of activities that is far more rich than the previous representation. All you need to do is to update the code that renders it in `recipes.php`, as shown in Example 4-19. You also can also take advantage of the profile icon that is returned with the attached user object.

Example 4-19. Display attempts from Google+ on the recipe page

```
<section class="content attempts">
  <?php foreach ($attempts as $attempt) { ?>
  <div class="attempt">
    <?php if(isset($attempt['photo_url'])) { ?>
    <img class="attempt-photo" src="<?= $attempt['photo_url'] ?>" />
    <?php } ?>

    <h3>
      <a href="<?= $attempt['author']['url']?>">
        <img src="<?= $attempt['author']['image']['url']?>"/></a>
      <?= $attempt['author']['displayName'] ?>'s Attempt
      <a class="import-link" href="<?= $attempt['url'] ?>">imported from Google+</a>
    </h3>

    <p>
      <?= str_replace("\n", "<br/>\n", stripslashes($attempt['description'])) ?>
    </p>
    <div style="clear:both;"></div>
  </div>
  <?php } ?>
</section>
```

Reload Baking Disasters and use the new import feature to pull in some of your recent baking attempts. The resulting import should look like Figure 4-18.

Your modest PHP web application is better than ever. You have used the Google+ APIs for a simple sign-in solution. Knowing who is signed in has provided the tools that you

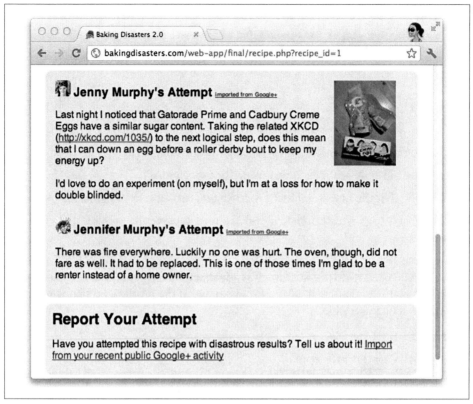

Figure 4-18. Two baking attempts imported from Google+

need to restrict administrative features to the correct users. You've also used the activity APIs to enable users import their recent adventures and associate them with a recipe. The way this integration was implemented has the added benefit of automatically updating the imported view when the canonical copy on Google+ is updated or deleted.

Additional endpoints exist for searching activities, listing people who took action on a specific activity and viewing comments. You can use these same techniques to add functionality that pulls data from these endpoints.

A Preview of the History API

The same developer preview for the sign-in button also includes a write API for Google+ called the history API. This API allows your application to write moments that represent your user's activity to a private place on Google+. Later your user can share the moments that are important to them with the right people on Google+.

Signing up for this developer preview follows the same process as for the sign-in button. Complete the sign-up form (*https://developers.google.com/*) and your account will be able to create API projects that use the history API and write moments to your Google history. You can also see these moments in a beta version of the Google+ history user interface at *https://plus.google.com/history*.

Each write to the history API has two parts: an HTTP POST and a publicly accessible target page with schema.org structured markup. The POST body, shown in Example 4-20, describes the type of activity that has occurred. It includes the URL of the entity that was the target of the activity and a JSON representation of any content created as the result of the activity.

Example 4-20. A CommentActivity

```
{
  "type": "http://schemas.google.com/CommentActivity", ❶
  "target": { ❷
    "url": "https://developers.google.com/+/plugins/snippet/examples/blog-entry"
  },
  "result": { ❸
    "type": "http://schema.org/Comment",
    "url": "https://developers.google.com/+/plugins/snippet/examples/blog-entry#comment-1",
    "name": "This is amazing!",
    "text": "I can't wait to use it on my site :)"
  }
}
```

❶ The type of activity that has been performed. This must be one of the types predefined by Google.

❷ The publicly accessible URL of the entity upon which the activity occurred.

❸ If the activity created content, a JSON representation of that data.

The target page, specified in the POST by target.url, is the second part of the moment write. It is fetched when the moment is written. This fetch extracts schema.org markup and includes it into the moment.

If you have already added schema.org markup to your pages for other social plugins like the +1 button, you will not need to make any additional changes to them.

> The history API is currently in developer preview. Expect rapid changes. Expect these changes to break your code.
>
> Please see the documentation (*https://developers.google.com/+/history*) to see the latest starter projects, reference docs, and implementation advice.

The developer preview of the history API provides a rare opportunity. Google is very interested in feedback from developers as they experiment with the APIs. For example, there is a pre-populated form for requesting new moment types: *https://developers.goo gle.com/+/history/api/moments#request_a_new_type*. If you request a moment type or change to the API during the developer preview it is much more likely to be incorporated into the released API.

Best Practices

For the sake of simplicity and ease of understanding the example code presented so far has cut some corners. For example, code has been copied and pasted in many places and it is not as efficient as it could be. Here are some tips to help guide you through efficient usage of the API.

Cache

> The code presented above creates client libraries and often uses them only once. Cache client libraries. They can be reused. Leverage caches for API requests too. Most of the client libraries take care of this for you, but you should still make sure that the client library is configured to cached data appropriately for your project. For example, the PHP client library provides four different cache implementations, one of which may work better for you.

Be paranoid

> Don't trust anyone when it comes to cross site scripting. Be very cautious when rendering input that comes from a user, even if it's coming via a Google API. Escape everything. The implementation of these practices will differ a bit on your language and platform.

CHAPTER 5

Collaborative Baking with Hangout Apps

Google+ Hangouts provide an easy way to create 10-way video conferences. This is a pretty cool feature on its own, but with the Hangout API you can extend them.

You can author your own JavaScript applications that have access to a data structure that is automatically synchronized between all participants in the hangout. You can also programmatically manipulate many aspects of the running hangout environment, including adding image overlays to the video streams of hangout participants.

Potluck Party Planner

As fun as it is to experiment alone, inviting friends takes baking disasters to the next level. You can distribute the cost of your baking party by making it an ingredient potluck. Your baking friends can each volunteer to bring some of the ingredients for the recipe that you're going to attempt together.

The process of deciding who will bring what is highly collaborative. It's a perfect case for a Hangout App. This is a great opportunity to extend your baking disasters web application into a hangout with a Potluck Party Planner app.

Potluck Party Planner allows the hangout participants to select a recipe that they wish to attempt. Next, a list of ingredients is displayed. Participants can then volunteer to bring an ingredient to the party by clicking it. The participant who has agreed to bring the most ingredients is rewarded with a virtual chef's hat made possible by a media overlay. Finally, participants share a reminder to Google+ with a list of the ingredients that they have volunteered to bring. The flow is shown in Figure 5-1.

Figure 5-1. Users select a recipe to bake → users volunteer to bring ingredients and the top volunteer is provided a chef's hat → users share their shopping list to Google+

Architecture of a Hangout App

A Hangout Application consists of three parts, as shown in Figure 5-2: a `gadget.xml` specification file, JavaScript for the real-time interaction, and optional server-side APIs. These APIs allow your hangout application to access data that resides outside the hangout.

Hosting a Hangout App

You're probably eager to dive into the code, but to save headaches later you need to take care of a few things first. There are special considerations you must take into account when hosting them.

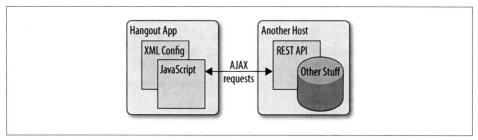

Figure 5-2. A typical Hangout App architecture featuring XML configuration, JavaScript that runs within the hangout, and REST APIs on a remote system

The sample applications provided by Google all run on Google App Engine. App Engine provides a great place to host Hangout Apps, but it does not support PHP and hence can't run Baking Disasters. To achieve tight integration between your web application and Hangout App you will need to make some changes. You'll need to serve files over SSL and configure cache control headers.

SSL is a must both during development and later when your application is in production. Hangouts themselves run in SSL. You're free to create hangout apps that include content served over unencrypted HTTP, but web browsers do not like it when you do this. Even in web browsers configured with the default security settings you'll see mixed content warnings and even errors resulting from files failing to load.

You must serve your static files and API requests over SSL. There are a few ways to do this. If you're running on a subdomain of a shared domain from your provider, as is the case with Google App Engine's appspot.com, you can leverage their existing wildcard SSL certificate. If that's not available or you are running on your own domain, you'll need to purchase and install an SSL certificate.

If this is a lengthy process, there is an alternative that you can use during development. You can use a self-signed SSL certificate and force your web browser or operating system to trust it.

In addition to being able to serve content over SSL, you should have control over the HTTP cache headers. While you develop your hangout application you're going to be going through the familiar code, deploy, and test loop. In fact, you're going to be doing it quite rapidly. The hangout APIs will respect cache directives in serving these files. This means that the default cache directives set by your web server will probably make development quite cumbersome. While you are developing your application you should disable caching, but don't forget to then it back on when you're ready to release your application to the world!

With these two issues taken care of, you're ready to build.

Starting with a Starter Project

Now that you know what you're going to build and where you're going to host the code, it's time to start hacking. Starter apps are a great place to start, and the Hangouts API is no different. As mentioned above, the Google-provided sample applications are all intended to be hosted on Google App Engine, but with a few tweaks you can convert them to your PHP environment.

Convert the Starter Project to PHP

Download a copy of the starter app from the hangouts sample apps page: *https://devel opers.google.com/+/hangouts/sample-apps*. This archive contains several files, as shown in Figure 5-3.

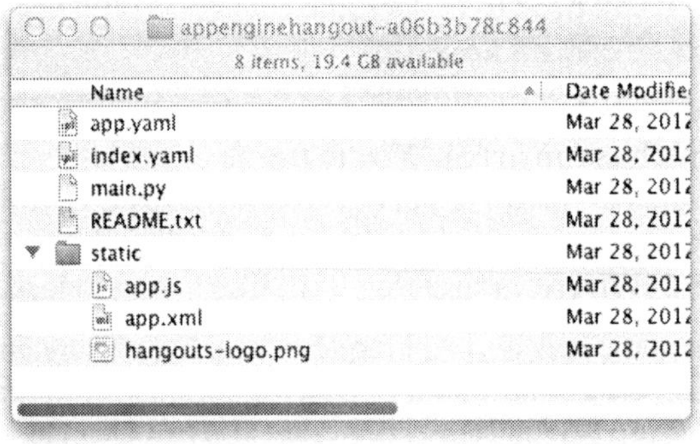

Figure 5-3. The contents of the Hangout API starter project

Two YAML files contain App Engine configuration. Because we're not running on App Engine, you can ignore them. The `app.js` and `app.xml` files in the static folder contain most of the Hangout App code. Following the instructions in the included readme, update the URLs inside of them to refer to your web host.

The initial contents of `app.js` in Example 5-1 become Example 5-2, and so on elsewhere in the starter project files.

Example 5-1. The initial contents of app.js

```
var serverPath = '//YOUR_APP_ID.appspot.com/';

function countButtonClick() {
```

Example 5-2. app.js with a server path specified

```
var serverPath = '//bakingdisasters.com/potluck-party-planner/hangoutstarter/';

function countButtonClick() {
```

Next, open `main.py`. As shown in Example 5-3, this file contains a simple AJAX handler.

Example 5-3. A simple AJAX handler in Python for App Engine

```
class MainHandler(webapp.RequestHandler):
    def get(self):
        # Set the cross origin resource sharing header to allow AJAX
        self.response.headers.add_header("Access-Control-Allow-Origin", "*")
        # Print some JSON
        self.response.out.write('{"message":"Hello World!"}\n')


def main():
    application = webapp.WSGIApplication([('/', MainHandler)],
                                         debug=True)
    util.run_wsgi_app(application)

if __name__ == '__main__':
    main()
```

Reproducing it in PHP is easy. Create a file named `index.php` in the root of your project with the code in Example 5-4.

Example 5-4. The same AJAX handler written in PHP

```
<?php
header("Access-Control-Allow-Origin: *"); ❶
header("Content-type: application/json"); ❷
?>
{"message":"Hello World!"}
```

❶ A simple cross-origin resource sharing header to make cross domain requests easier. If you host your `app.js` file on the same domain as `index.php`, this is not strictly necessary.

❷ By default PHP sets a `text/html` content type. Override it because this file responds with JSON.

Finally, deploy the updated starter project to your web host.

Run the Starter Project

There is one last step that you must complete to run the Hangout App starter project. You must enable the Hangouts API on the Baking Disasters API console project. Follow these steps to configure your API console project and start the hangout in development mode.

1. Return to the service panel for Baking Disasters on the API console: *https://devel opers.google.com/console#:services*.

2. Enable the hangouts API on the services panel by toggling the switch to *ON* as shown in Figure 5-4.

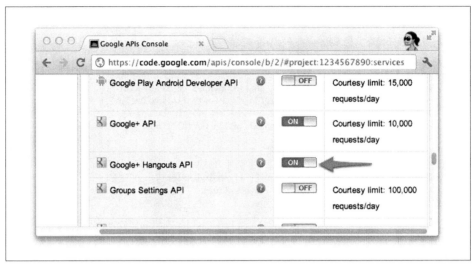

Figure 5-4. Enabling the Google+ Hangouts API on the API console

3. Switch to the newly revealed Hangouts panel shown in Figure 5-5. Paste the URL for your deployed `app.xml` into the Application URL field.

4. Scroll to the bottom of the page, as shown in Figure 5-6. Click Save and then the *Enter a hangout* link to initiate a development mode hangout running your starter project.

5. If you're asked about permissions, grant them to allow the hangout app to start.

The application, shown in Figure 5-7, is quite simple. It consists of a count that is synchronized across all users, and a *Get Message* button, which uses AJAX to fetch the response from `index.php`.

Alongside the features contained in your starter project there are a some development tools. The *Reset app state* button deletes the contents of the shared state, and the *Reload app* button reloads the app's html and JavaScript, but it does not clear the shared state. If you are not careful with your code, using these buttons independently may result in some unusual behavior.

To fully experience the starter application, now is a good time to recruit a friend to join your hangout. Since your application is still in development mode, you must add your collaborators to your development team on the API console. You can use the team panel, shown in Figure 5-8 of the API console to add your collaborators: *https://devel opers.google.com/console#:team*

Once you have added them to your project, restart your hangout and invite them to join you.

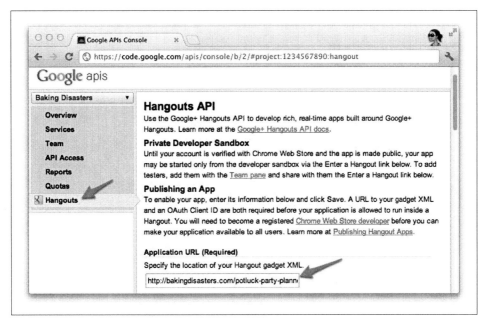

Figure 5-5. Associating the deployed app.xml file in the API console

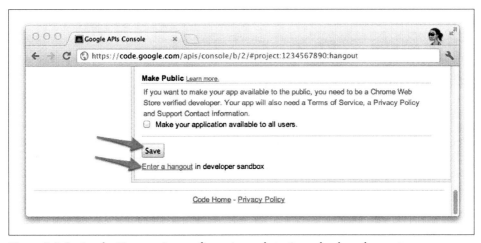

Figure 5-6. Saving the Hangout App configuration and starting a developer hangout

As simple as the starter app is, it contains basic usage of all of the APIs that you will need to write the potluck planner app. It uses the shared state and callbacks to maintain the synchronized count and makes AJAX calls to APIs hosted server side.

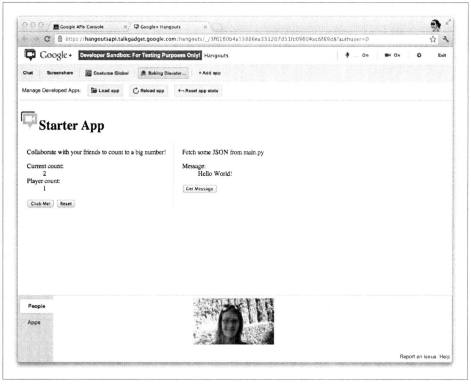

Figure 5-7. Running the Hangout API starter app

Collaborative Planning

The starter project provides a solid foundation. It's time to mold it into the potluck party planner. Taking a bottom-up approach this involves enhancing the AJAX handler to communicate recipes and ingredients, modifying the HTML in `app.xml`, and then adding JavaScript to synchronize participant state and manipulate the HTML. This design is shown in Figure 5-9.

Once the core interaction features are implemented, you can loop back and add enhancements like the ingredient reminder sharing and the chef's hat overlay for the top contributor.

Recipe and Ingredient REST APIs

The hangout app needs data from Baking Disasters to function. Specifically, it needs access to a list of all available recipes and a way to list the ingredients required for each of those recipes.

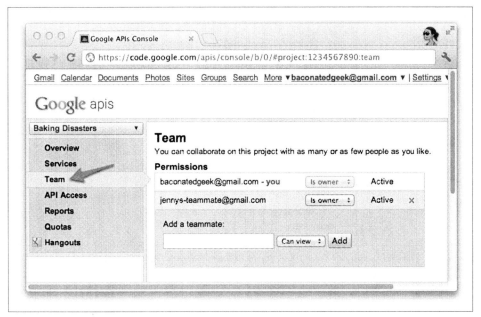

Figure 5-8. Adding project team members on the API console

REST APIs are a great way to communicate data to AJAX applications. Implementing simple REST APIs is quite easy in PHP. Create a new file, `api.php`. Start by adding some headers to turn this php file into a REST API, as shown in Example 5-5.

Example 5-5. HTTP headers that allow a PHP file to be used as an AJAX handler

```php
<?php
header("Access-Control-Allow-Origin: *");
header("Content-type: application/json");

include_once("util.php");
```

Use GET parameters to control which data you will return. If recipes is set, you know that the hangout is asking for a list of all available recipes, so fetch them from the database, convert, and print them into the response, as shown in Example 5-6.

Example 5-6. Print a list of all recipes as JSON

```php
if ($_GET['recipes']) {
  $recipes = list_recipes();
  $response = array();

  foreach ($recipes as $recipe) {
    array_push($response, array(
      'id'=>$recipe['rowid'],
      'name'=>$recipe['name'],
      'imageUrl'=>$recipe['photo_url']
```

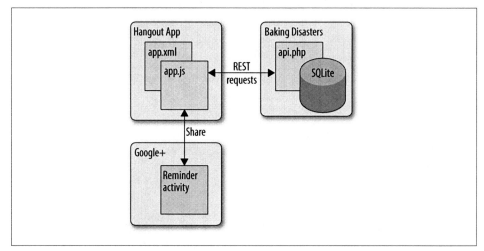

Figure 5-9. The architecture of the Potluck Party Planner Hangout App.

```
    ));
  }
}
```

If ingredients is set, use the id parameter to look up the ingredients for that recipe and respond with them in the same way, as shown in Example 5-7.

Example 5-7. Print a list of ingredients for a recipe as JSON

```php
} else if ($_GET['ingredients']) {
    $recipe = get_recipe($_GET['id']);
    if($recipe) {
      $response = array(
        'name'=>$recipe['name'],
        'ingredients'=>explode("\r\n", $recipe['ingredients']));
      echo str_replace('\/', '/', json_encode($response));
  }
}
```

And finally, fall through to a simple error if neither are set, as shown in Example 5-8.

Example 5-8. Respond to all other requests with a 404 status code

```php
} else {
  header("HTTP/1.0 404 Not Found");
  echo '{"error":"not found"}';
}
```

This single file API provides all of the data access that the hangout application needs.

In practice on your application, the implementation of any APIs you provide will be different. If you're using an MVC framework, it probably provides an easy way to expose entities in your application as simple APIs.

Hangout App Interface

Hangout apps, at their core, are HTML web applications that run inside of an iframe. All user interaction is made through HTML. The initial state of this HTML is specified inside the app.xml file and manipulated as the app runs by JavaScript.

The potluck party planner has two screens: one for recipe selection and another for ingredient selection. An easy way to model this is to create both screens within the initial HTML. Use CSS to hide them at startup and then use JavaScript to display at the right time.

Merge the header from Baking Disasters into app.xml to provide a foundation for further features. Example 5-9 shows the result of this merger.

Example 5-9. The result of merging the Baking Disasters layout with the app.xml file from the Hangout Apps starter project

```
<!DOCTYPE html>
<html>
<head>
  <title>Baking Disasters 2.0</title>
  <script src="//hangoutsapi.talkgadget.google.com/hangouts/api/hangout.js?v=1.0">
  </script>
  <script src="//bakingdisasters.com/potluck-party-planner/final/app.js?foo=bar">
  </script>
  <script src="//apis.google.com/js/plusone.js"></script>
  <link rel="stylesheet"
    href="//bakingdisasters.com/potluck-party-planner/final/style.css"/>
  <link rel="shortcut icon"
    href="//bakingdisasters.com/potluck-party-planner/final/images/logo_favicon.png" />
</head>
<body>
<header class="blog-header">
  <img id="blog-logo"
    src="//bakingdisasters.com/potluck-party-planner/final/images/logo.png"/>
  <h1>Baking Disasters</h1>
  <p>Because sometimes molecular gastronomy explodes.</p>
</header>
  <section class="content">
  </section>
<footer>
  By <a href="http://plus.google.com/116852994107721644038">Baking Disasters</a>
</footer>
</body>
</html>
```

With this foundation created add some content panes. The design calls to start with a list of recipes, but calling the recipe list API may take some time so start with a content panel that displays a loading message, as shown in Example 5-10.

Example 5-10. A loading message that is displayed while the Hangout App starts up

```
<section class="content" id="loading">
  <p>Hang in there! Stuff is still loading.</p>
</section>
```

Once the app has finished loading it should display a list of recipes. Create a section for this but make it hidden by default, as shown in Example 5-11.

Example 5-11. HTML for an empty recipe list

```
<section class="content" id="recipe-list-content" style="display: none;"> ❶
  <h2>Potluck Planner</h2>
  <p>Select a recipe for your potluck:</p>
  <ul id="recipe-list"></ul> ❷
  <div style="clear: both;"></div>
</section>
```

❶ The `display: none;` CSS prevents this section from being visible.

❷ Recipes render within the `recipe-list` list.

And finally, once the recipe has been selected, users need a way to volunteer to bring ingredients. The HTML for the ingredients panel is shown in Example 5-12.

Example 5-12. HTML for an empty ingredients list

```
<section class="content" id="ingredient-list-content" style="display: none;">
  <h2>
    <a href="javascript:recipeUnselect()">&larr;</a>
    Recipe selected: <span id="recipe-name"></span>
  </h2>
  <p>Select stuff to bring:</p>
  <table class="who-bring-what">
    <thead>
      <tr><th>Who</th><th>What</th></tr>
    </thead>
    <tbody id="claim-list"> ❶
    </tbody>
    </table>
  </section>
```

❶ Ingredients render within the `claim-list` element of the `who-bring-what` table.

JavaScript is the glue that puts this interface and the Baking Disasters REST APIs together, in a hangout.

You can put JavaScript in `app.xml` too, but it quickly becomes cumbersome. It's easier to break it out into a separate file. Create a new file, `app.js`, and include it into the head element, as shown in Example 5-13.

Example 5-13. Including app.js into app.xml

```
<script src="//bakingdisasters.com/potluck-party-planner/final/app.js"></script>
```

Hangout App Startup

When the hangout starts up, Potluck Party Planner must be initialized to render the list of recipes that available for selection. The Hangout API can be configured to call a function once loading is complete using the function shown in Example 5-14.

Example 5-14. Registering an init function

```
gadgets.util.registerOnLoadHandler(init);
```

Within the `init` function you register a callback that executes when the Hangout API has finished its own initialization. Within this function you can register other callbacks, as shown in Example 5-15. In an application as simple as this one, you can funnel the initialization and other callbacks into a single `updateUi` function, as shown in Example 5-16.

Example 5-15. Registering more specific callbacks within the init function

```
function init() {
  var apiReady = function(eventObj) {
    if (eventObj.isApiReady) { ❶

      // set up the handlers for callback from the hangout
      gapi.hangout.data.onStateChanged.add(function(eventObj) { ❷
        updateUi();
      });
      gapi.hangout.onParticipantsChanged.add(function(eventObj) { ❸
        updateUi();
      });

      // Render the initial interface
      updateUi(); ❹

      gapi.hangout.onApiReady.remove(apiReady); ❺
    }
  };
  gapi.hangout.onApiReady.add(apiReady); ❻
}
```

❻ Register the `apiReady` function to execute when the Hangouts API is ready for instructions.

❶ Wait for the API to become fully ready.

❷ Update the user interface whenever the shared state changes.

❸ Update the user interface when participants join or leave the hangout.

❹ Render the initial user interface.

❺ Remove the `apiReady` callback to ensure that it does not run again.

Initially, the function shown in Example 5-17 renders the recipe list.

Example 5-16. One function to handle all interface updates

```
function updateUi() {
  renderRecipes();
}
```

Example 5-17. Render the list of recipes fetched from app.php into the empty recipes list and make it visible

```
function renderRecipes() {
  // Toggle the recipe list to on
  document.getElementById("loading").style.display = "none"; ❶
  document.getElementById("ingredient-list-content").style.display = "none";
  document.getElementById("recipe-list-content").style.display = "block";

  var recipes = getRecipes(); ❷

  var recipeList = document.getElementById("recipe-list");
  recipeList.innerHTML = ""; ❸
  for (var i in recipes) { ❹
    var recipeElement = document.createElement("li");
    var recipeImage = document.createElement("img");
    recipeImage.src = recipes[i].imageUrl;
    recipeElement.appendChild(recipeImage);
    recipeElement.appendChild(document.createTextNode(recipes[i].name));
    recipeElement.id = "recipe_" + recipes[i].id;
    recipeElement.addEventListener("click", recipeSelect, false);
    recipeList.appendChild(recipeElement);
  }
}
```

❶ Toggle the interface to display the recipe list section and hide everything else.

❷ Fetch the list of recipes from the simple API on Baking Disasters.

❸ Clear the current recipe list if any. It may have since the last invocation.

❹ Create HTML elements for the recipes and insert them into the recipe list.

Shared State and HTML Manipulations

The most important function of `app.js` is to respond to participant actions and to update everyone's user interface. The Hangout API's shared state API takes care of the heavy lifting. All you need to do is update the state in response to user actions and it will automatically trigger callbacks in every participant's app. This includes the participant who triggered took the original action. The recommended sequence is shown in Figure 5-10.

> It is important that you never update the shared state from a function that is directly or indirectly executed as the result of a state change. This results in an infinite loop.

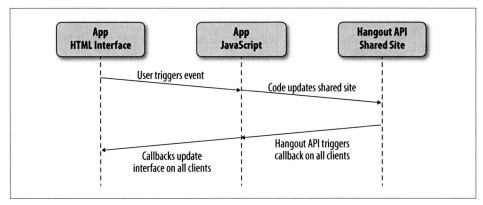

Figure 5-10. The update flow for shared state

Participants can take three possible actions when using potluck party planner. They can select or unselect a recipe and they can volunteer to bring an ingredient. The interface HTML already has JavaScript methods specified for these actions, so all you need to do is fill in the implementations.

Recipe selection, shown in Example 5-18, happens first. When a participant clicks on a recipe, the hangout app determines the recipe that they selected. Next, it makes an API call to Baking Disasters to fetch the ingredients for that recipe.

Once all of the important details about the selected recipe are known, you can update the shared state by calling gapi.hangout.data.submitDelta(). The shared state can only store strings, though, so all complex data, like the ingredients list, must be converted into a string to be stored.

Example 5-18. Respond to user clicks on a recipe in the list

```
function recipeSelect() {
  var recipeId = this.id.split("_")[1];
  var ingredientResponse = getIngredients(recipeId); ❶

  var delta = {'recipeName':ingredientResponse.name}; ❷
  var ingredients = new Array();
  for(var i in ingredientResponse.ingredients) {
    ingredients.push({"claimedBy":null, "ingredient":ingredientResponse.ingredients[i]});
  }
  delta['ingredients'] = JSON.stringify(ingredients); ❸

  gapi.hangout.data.submitDelta(delta); ❹
}
```

❶ Fetch the ingredients list for this recipe from the simple API.

❷ Gather up all changes to the shared state into a single local variable.

❸ Convert arrays and objects into strings to store them in the shared state.

❹ Submit the updates using submitDelta.

Use submitDelta() whenever multiple keys are updated rather than many calls to setValue(). Shared state updates are limited to several updates per second, but submitDelta() only counts as one call.

Unselecting recipes is much simpler. No data needs to be fetched from any API. Simply clear the ingredients list from the shared state using the gapi.hangout.data.clear Value() function, as shown in Example 5-19.

Example 5-19. Return to the recipes list by clearing the ingredients list

```
function recipeUnselect() {
  gapi.hangout.data.clearValue('ingredients');
}
```

When the shared state has been updated, the Hangouts API will trigger the callback function you registered earlier. Update this function to render the correct panel based on the new value in the shared state, as shown in Example 5-20.

Example 5-20. An expanded UI updated function that decides which list to display

```
function updateUi() {
  if (gapi.hangout.data.getValue('ingredients') == null) { ❶
    renderRecipes();
  } else {
    renderIngredients();
  }
}
```

❶ If there is no ingredient set in the shared state, display the recipe list.

Volunteering for ingredients follows a very similar flow, except since only one value is updated in the shared state, gapi.hangout.data.setValue() is sufficient.

Example 5-21. Respond to user clicks on ingredients

```
function ingredientSelect() {
  var claimId = this.id.split("_")[1];

  var ingredients = JSON.parse(gapi.hangout.data.getValue('ingredients')); ❶
  ingredients[claimId].claimedBy = gapi.hangout.getParticipantId(); ❷

  gapi.hangout.data.setValue('ingredients', JSON.stringify(ingredients)); ❸
}
```

❶ Recall the ingredients list from the shared state.

❷ Update the claimant for the target ingredient.

❸ Store the updated ingredient list back into the shared state.

The basic flow is ready for testing. Deploy the code and start a hangout. It will look something like Figure 5-11. You and your friends can select a recipe and volunteer for ingredients together.

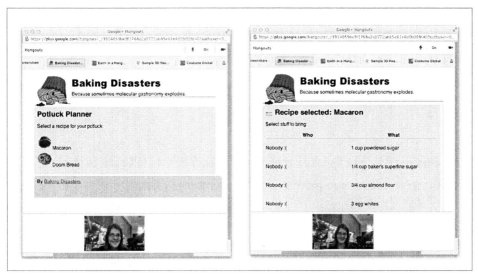

Figure 5-11. Potluck party planner running in a hangout: Left: The recipe selection panel; Right: The ingredient selection panel

Add Reminder Sharing

As it's implemented, the final list of ingredients that each person selected is lost at the end of the hangout. The share link can help close this loop by allowing participants to post a reminder to Google+.

Content that is posted to Google+ must have a publicly accessible URL. A simple way to implement this is to create a `reminder.php` file, as shown in Example 5-22. It accepts reminder text as a GET parameter and formats it for sharing on Google+ with schema.org markup.

Example 5-22. A PHP page that displays reminders, which are passed in via a GET parameter

```
<!DOCTYPE html>
<html>
<head>
  <title>Baking Disasters 2.0</title>
  <link rel="stylesheet" href="style.css"/>
  <link rel="shortcut icon" href="images/logo_favicon.png" />
</head>
<body>
<header class="blog-header">
  <a href="index.php"><img id="blog-logo" src="images/logo.png"/></a>
```

```
  <h1>Baking Disasters</h1>
  <p>Because sometimes molecular gastronomy explodes.</p>
</header>
<section class="content"  itemscope itemtype="http://schema.org/Thing"> ❶
  <h2 itemprop="name">Potluck Reminder</h2>
  <p>Remember to bring:</p>
  <pre itemprop="description">
<?= htmlspecialchars(urldecode($_GET["reminder"]), ENT_QUOTES, 'UTF-8'); ?> ❷
  </pre>
  <div style="clear: both;"></div>
</section>
<footer>
  By <a href="http://plus.google.com/116852994107721644038">Baking Disasters</a>
</footer>
</body>
</html>
```

❶ Schema.org does not specify a schema for a reminder, so fall back to thing.

❷ Use `htmlspecialchars` to prevent cross-site scripting issues.

 For large ingredient lists, this implementation will produce very large URLs. A more robust implementation might involve POSTing a reminder and creating a shareable URL that refers to that reminder by ID.

Wiring `reminder.php` into the hangout app involves adding a place for the share link to render and rendering a share link with the GET parameter populated by the current ingredient list.

Add a placeholder reminder button to `app.xml` in the head element of the interface HTML, as shown in Example 5-23.

Example 5-23. A placeholder share link

```
<a style="display: none;" id="reminder-share-link"
href="https://plus.google.com/share?url=http://bakingdisasters.com">
  Share a shopping reminder on <img
  src="https://www.gstatic.com/images/icons/gplus-16.png"
  alt="Share a shopping reminder on Google+"/></a>
```

Next, add a function to `app.js` that updates the placeholder reminder link to share the list of ingredients that the current user has committed to bring, as shown in Example 5-24.

Example 5-24. JavaScript that updates the share link to the participants ingredient list

```
function renderReminderButton() {
  var ingredients = JSON.parse(gapi.hangout.data.getValue('ingredients')); ❶
  var participantId = gapi.hangout.getParticipantId();
  var reminderText = gapi.hangout.getParticipantById(participantId).person.displayName;
  reminderText += " will bring: ";
```

```
  for (var i in ingredients) {
    if(ingredients[i].claimedBy == participantId) {
      reminderText += ingredients[i].ingredient + "%0A"; ❷
    }
  }
  if(reminderText.length > 0) {
    var reminderShareLink = document.getElementById("reminder-share-link");

    var reminderUrl = "https://plus.google.com/share?url=" + ❸
      encodeURIComponent(BACKEND_BASE_URI + "/reminder.php?reminder=" +
        encodeURIComponent(reminderText));

    reminderShareLink.href = reminderUrl; ❹

    reminderShareLink.onclick = function() { ❺
      window.open(reminderUrl, '',
        'menubar=no,toolbar=no,resizable=yes,scrollbars=yes,height=600,width=600');
    };

    reminderShareLink.style.display = "inline"; ❻
  }
}
```

❶ Recall the ingredients list from the shared state.

❷ Crudely URL-encode the list of ingredients claimed by the current participant.

❸ Construct the share link URL.

❹ Update the `href` attribute of the reminder link to point to the share link URL.

❺ Add a JavaScript callback to open the share link in a new window.

❻ Display the share link if it is still hidden.

This share link must be updated in response to ingredient selection. Add it to the `updateUi()` function, as shown in Example 5-25.

Example 5-25. The updateUi function enhanced to add the reminder share link.

```
function updateUi() {
  // If there's no ingredient state, display the recipes list
  if (gapi.hangout.data.getValue('ingredients') == null) {
    renderRecipes();
  } else {
    renderIngredients();
    renderReminderButton();
  }
}
```

The next time you run the hangout, a reminder link will appear. Clicking on the reminder link will bring up a share window. Share it with yourself, or whoever does your grocery shopping. An example reminder is shown in Figure 5-12.

Figure 5-12. Left, a share window rendered from a share link in the Potluck Party Planner; right, the resulting activity on Google+

Media APIs

The shared state APIs provide you everything you need to get the job done, but hangouts are supposed to be fun. You can use the media APIs to make the application a little more fun and provide an incentive for users to volunteer to bring ingredients: during ingredient selection, the user who has volunteered to bring the greatest number of ingredients to the party will be rewarded with a chef's hat that appears in their thumbnail to everyone in the hangout.

Media overlays are created from images and later attached to a user's face with a different API call. You can create media overlays dynamically with any URI, even a data URI, but this use case can be satisfied by reusing a single overlay. Create the overlay at startup from a static image and store it into a global variable for use later, as shown in Example 5-26.

Example 5-26. Create a chef's hat overlay during initialization and store it into a global variable

```
var chefHatOverlay; ❶
...
function createHatOverlay() { ❷
  var chefHat = gapi.hangout.av.effects.createImageResource(
    BACKEND_BASE_URI + '/images/chef_hat.png');
  chefHatOverlay = chefHat.createFaceTrackingOverlay(
    {'trackingFeature':
      gapi.hangout.av.effects.FaceTrackingFeature.NOSE_ROOT,
      'scaleWithFace': true,
      'rotateWithFace': true,
      'scale': 4,
      'offset': {x: 0, y: -0.3}});
}
```

❶ Use a global variable to store the overlay.

❷ Create the overlay by calling `createHatOverlay` from `init`.

This code specifies some seemingly arbitrary values for the attachment point, scale, and offset. These parameters behave consistently, but it's usually easiest to guess some reasonable values for your image and make adjustments to the working application.

Now that you have an overlay to apply, you must tell the app when to render it. The app already has an updateUI() function that updates the interface after a user selects an ingredient. Use the same logic to trigger the assignment of the chef's hat, as shown in Example 5-27.

Example 5-27. Recalculate the chef's hat assignment within the updateUi+ function

```
function updateUi() {
  // If there's no ingredient state, display the recipes list
  if (gapi.hangout.data.getValue('ingredients') == null) {
    renderRecipes();
  } else {
    renderIngredients();
    assignChefHat();
    renderReminderButton();
  }
}
```

Each time an ingredient is selected you can inspect the shared state to determine the participant who has volunteered to bring the greatest number of ingredients. Next, loop through the participants, assign the hat to the top contributor and clear out the hats worn by everyone else. Example 5-28 shows how to do this.

Example 5-28. Determine the leading participant and assign them the chef's hat

```
function assignChefHat() {
  var ingredients = JSON.parse(gapi.hangout.data.getValue('ingredients')); ❶
  var totals = new Array();

  for(var i in ingredients) { ❷
    var ingredient = ingredients[i];
    var person = ingredient.claimedBy;
    if(person != null) {
      if(totals[person]) {
        totals[person]++;
      } else {
        totals[person] = 1;
      }
    }
  }

  var hatOwner = null;
  var currentMax = 0;
  for(person in totals) {
    if(totals[person] > currentMax) {
      currentMax = totals[person];
      hatOwner = person;
    }
  }
```

```
    console.log(hatOwner + " gets the hat with total of " + currentMax);

  if(hatOwner == gapi.hangout.getParticipantId()) { ❸
    chefHatOverlay.setVisible(true);
  } else {
    chefHatOverlay.setVisible(false);
  }
}
```

❶ Recall the ingredients list from the shared state.

❷ Determine the participant who has claimed the greatest number of ingredients.

❸ Display the chef's hat if the current participant claimed the most ingredients.

Deploy the code, start a hangout, and select a few ingredients to see a chef's hat render above your head, as shown in Figure 5-13.

In this exercise you applied a media overlay. The media APIs provide other features that may be useful in your application. You can play sounds in the hangout. The sound APIs leverage the noise-canceling features of the hangout to ensure they are only heard by the correct participants. You can also affix images to the thumbnail view itself instead of the participants' faces. You can even access the coordinates of the participants' facial features programmatically. You can learn more about the available media API methods in the Hangout API reference documentation: *https://developers.google.com/+/hang outs/api/gapi.hangout.av.effects*

Other Hangout APIs

The Hangouts API is quite broad. It has many other methods and callbacks related to other hangout features. You can change the state of cameras and microphones, make your app react to changes in the On Air broadcast state of the hangout, and even embed video feeds into your main application pane. The best way to explore these features is to pursue the API reference documentation: *https://developers.google.com/+/hangouts/api/gapi.hangout*

Publishing

Now that you have a working hangout application, it's time to allow people outside of your development team to use it. Follow these steps to make your hangout app public.

1. Return to the API console, *https://developers.google.com/console*.

2. Open the Hangouts panel for your application.

3. Provide URLs for the Privacy Policy, Terms of Service, and Contact fields.

4. Create a Chrome Web Store account and verify it by paying a one-time $5 fee, as shown in Figure 5-14.

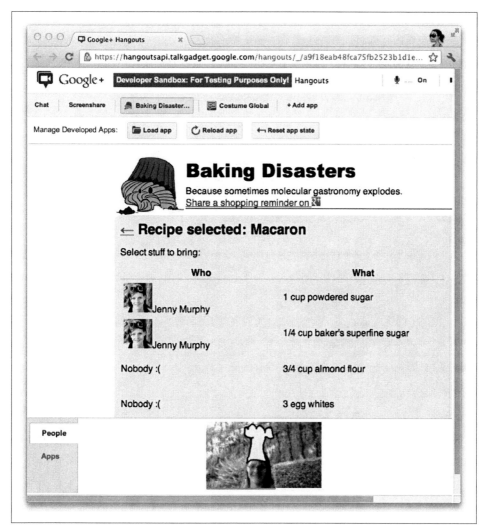

Figure 5-13. Potluck Party Planner rendering a chef's hat on Jenny's head

5. Check the published checkbox on the API console, shown in Figure 5-15, and click *Save*.

6. Create and add the hangout button to your website. Start by copying your application ID from the URL in the address bar on the API console, as shown in Figure 5-16.

7. Create a button with that ID. The resulting markup is shown in Example 5-29.

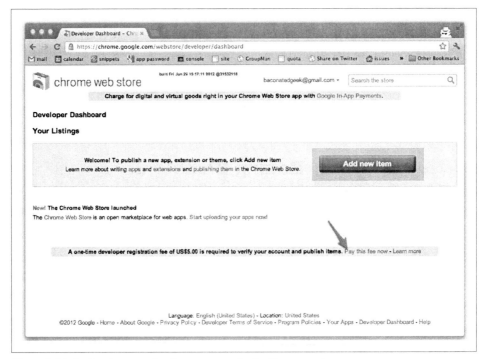

Figure 5-14. Registering your developer account in the Chrome web store

Figure 5-15. Publishing your hangout app

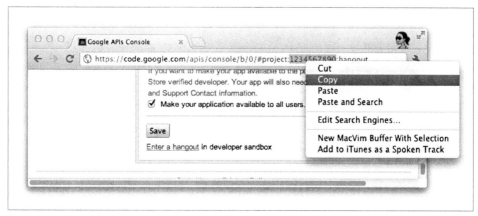

Figure 5-16. Copying the project ID from the URL on the API console

Example 5-29. HTML markup for a hangout button

```
<a href="https://plus.google.com/hangouts/_?gid=1234567890"
  style="text-decoration:none;">
  <img
src="https://ssl.gstatic.com/s2/oz/images/stars/hangout/1/gplus-hangout-20x86-normal.png"
    alt="Start a Hangout"
    style="border:0;width:86px;height:20px;"/>
</a>
```

Add it to a webpage, such as the Baking Disasters main index as shown in Figure 5-17, and click the button to start a hangout.

Use the built in hangout invitation features to invite your friends. You can now plan your potluck disaster.

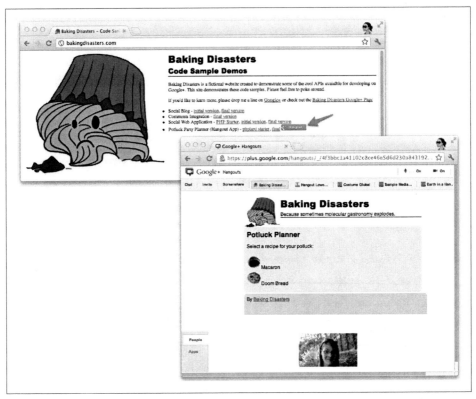

Figure 5-17. Using the Hangout button to initiate a hangout running the potluck party planner

CHAPTER 6

Wrapping Up the Baked Goods

Over the course of this book you have enhanced a blog with social plugins, written a web application that uses Google+ for authentication and as a data source, created a hangout app to make potluck planning easier, and taken a sneak peak at the upcoming history API. You can find the latest source code for all of these projects at *http://code .google.com/p/baking-disasters/* and running examples at *https://bakingdisasters.com/*.

As you've completed these projects you've carved a path through the Google+ platform, but there are many other features to explore. As you explore you can find help in many places. As you start your project you can find configuration tools, starter projects, reference documentation and samples at *https://developers.google.com/+*. As your project evolves, you can find help overcoming the roadblocks that you encounter through many support channels such as hangout office hours, IRC chat, StackOverflow and a discussion forum. Links to these support resources can be found at *https://developers.goo gle.com/+/support*.

About the Author

Jennifer works in Developer Relations on social products at Google. Previously she has worked in a wide variety of software engineering roles, from robotics at NASA to the architect of a social media startup. She is passionate about writing and education, especially on the subjects of technology and science.

Get even more
for your money.

Join the O'Reilly Community, and register the O'Reilly books you own. It's free, and you'll get:

- $4.99 ebook upgrade offer
- 40% upgrade offer on O'Reilly print books
- Membership discounts on books and events
- Free lifetime updates to ebooks and videos
- Multiple ebook formats, DRM FREE
- Participation in the O'Reilly community
- Newsletters
- Account management
- 100% Satisfaction Guarantee

Signing up is easy:

1. **Go to: oreilly.com/go/register**
2. **Create an O'Reilly login.**
3. **Provide your address.**
4. **Register your books.**

Note: English-language books only

To order books online:

oreilly.com/store

For questions about products or an order:

orders@oreilly.com

To sign up to get topic-specific email announcements and/or news about upcoming books, conferences, special offers, and new technologies:

elists@oreilly.com

For technical questions about book content:

booktech@oreilly.com

To submit new book proposals to our editors:

proposals@oreilly.com

O'Reilly books are available in multiple DRM-free ebook formats. For more information:

oreilly.com/ebooks

Spreading the knowledge of innovators   oreilly.com